MICHAEL DAWSON

MASHMAKER

A CITIZEN-BREWER'S GUIDE
TO MAKING GREAT BEER
AT HOME

W0007623

ISBN 13: 978-1-63489-096-0

Library of Congress Catalog Number: 2017955403
Printed in the United States of America
First Printing: 2018

21 20 19181754321

Edited by John Garland
Cover design by Nick Zdon
Interior design by Andrew Welyczko
Illustrations by David Witt, Jeff Nelson
Copyediting by Kate Murphy
Production by Joseph Alton, Brian Kaufenberg

Publishing Consulting by Wise Ink Creative Publishing

GRAY DUCK MEDIA

Gray Duck Media
1095 7th. St. W.
St. Paul, MN 55102
www.grayduck.media

To order your copy, visit mashmakerbook.com.

Reseller discounts available. To order, visit www.itascabooks.com or call 1-800-901-3480.

RECIPES

Citizens,

Thank you and congratulations on not choosing the easy way.

There are much simpler, faster, and less messy avenues than home-brewing to fill an empty glass with beer. Just like there are simpler, faster, and less messy ways than gardening to get some sliced tomato, or tending a smoker for 16 hours to eat some brisket. Even though we're living in a world that puts a premium on convenience and immediate gratification, there's value for our mental health and well-being to participate in a process that's on its own biochemical timetable and that dates back to the earliest days of human civilization.

Plus, if you enjoy beer—and it's unlikely you're even reading this if you don't—brewing it yourself is an opportunity to interface with it a lot more, and more intimately.

This book is a collection of recipes which I've enjoyed developing and brewing over many years. They can be brewed as-is or modded (suggestions and jumping-off points are included) and tailored to your personal homebrew system and preferences. There are chapters on process and raw materials, which are by no means comprehensive but enough to get you going and carry on a conversation at elegant dinner parties and/or beer festivals.

There are a lot of people I would like to acknowledge, more than I can fit here. But I would like to single out my dad Larry Dawson, my homebrewing partner on my very first batches; Chris Farley, for giving me a start; Chip Walton and Jake Keeler for always getting things done in April; and to John Garland, Joe Alton, and the rest of the Growler team for making this whole thing possible.

Drink it like you brewed it,

Michael Dawson

MALT

Malt operates under a lot of metaphorical weight. It's called the soul, engine, backbone, and foundation of beer. All of which makes malt sound extremely important, and it is.

Malt supplies the sugars and nutrients that yeast will use during fermentation. It creates a beer's color and body, and a host of grain-related flavors and aromas. Variations in raw materials, and the malting process itself, result in a wide range of colors and organoleptic profiles, so malt gives brewers a huge palette with which to paint. Malt bills for a recipe can be made from a single type of malt or a laundry list, allowing us to create a galaxy of beers with an incredible diversity of sensory qualities.

Many types of grain can be used to make malt—sorghum, millet, wheat—but for most of the western world, it's barley. A few key characteristics have made barley most desirable as a brewing grain. It retains its husk after threshing, which is unusual among cereal grains, and this creates a natural filter medium when it comes time to separate the sweet wort from the mash. Its lower gluten content makes it less-well suited to baking than its cousin wheat, thus a neat division of labor grew over time between the two: one making bread, the other making the liquid variety. Barley is also well-adapted to a wide range of climates. For the past 10,000 years, it's been widely accessible to brewers from the Middle East to far northern Europe to the high elevations of South America.

Grain destined to become malt has to meet a number of fairly strict criteria—mere cattle feed won't do for transmogrifying into beer. The grain must be grown under conditions that yield a favorable nitrogen ratio (this is where the foam-positive proteins, amino acids, and

The Malting Process

Malting takes place in three steps over the span of several days:

1. Steeping (36 to 48 Hours)

Grain is directed into large steeping tanks filled with water at a temperature of 52-56°F. Air is injected into the water to maintain proper dissolved oxygen levels. A series of immersions is done to assure that the barley is completely washed and uniformly hydrated. During steeping, the moisture content of the grain will be raised from post-harvest levels of approximately 12 percent up to 44-45 percent.

2. Germination (96 Hours)

After steeping, the grain is gently transported to germination compartments. It is held under controlled temperature, water additions, airflow, and humidity for approximately four days. The grain's native enzymes are activated and the starches are broken down into more simple forms of sugars that can be assimilated by yeast during fermentation.

3. Kilning (24 to 36 hours)

The grain is now referred to as "green malt" and is moved into kilns, large rectangular or circular vessels with perforated floors, for drying. For base malt, the green malt is dried to 4 percent moisture using high volumes of air at temperatures up to 190°F. The air temperature and airflow are closely controlled to achieve the desired malt attributes.

Information courtesy of Rahr Malting Co.

enzymes originate.) High doses of herbicides, pesticides, and fertilizer in the field can inhibit or prevent critical stages of the malting and brewing processes, so malting grain must be grown without this kind or degree of intervention. Malting barley gives lower yields to the farmer than seed or feed crops, and is thus more expensive than the aforementioned cattle feed.

WHAT IS MALT?

Malt is the intermediate stage between the cereal grain in the field and the beer in your pint glass. To become malt, the starchy seed of a cereal grain has to undergo malting, a highly controlled and limited germination of the kernel or seed.

Several critical things are achieved by malting grain. First, it uses the native enzymes of the grain kernel to break down cell walls and access the kernel's food reserves—the starches that will become fermentable sugars in the mash—as well as free amino nitrogen (FAN), amino acids, and trace nutrients that the yeast cells will need. Secondly, it creates important organoleptic components like color, flavor, and aroma. Raw cereal tastes grainy, astringent, and not that interesting, but malting replaces all that with a range of flavors from pastry dough and bread crust, to chocolate and coffee. Finally, it makes the grain friable, or easily crushed. Raw grain is quite difficult to mill.

TYPES OF MALTS

Base Malts

Not base as in low or inferior, but base as in the foundation. These make up the bulk (if not all) of a beer's grist. Their job is to supply starches, the enzymes required to convert those starches to fermentable sugars, plus nutrients and flavor/aroma compounds. On their own, most base malts won't yield much color. Beers brewed with 100 percent base malt will usually be straw- to golden-colored, although those brewed with Vienna or Munich will venture into the orange and amber spectrum. Base malts include:

- **Pilsner malt:** A traditional base malt for many beer styles, particularly lagers. Typically very pale.

- **Pale ale malt:** Associated with ale brewing, it usually has a more robust flavor and a bit more color than Pilsner malt.

- **Vienna malt:** Kilned to a higher color than Pils or pale, it yields a pale orange wort with a subtle biscuit flavor.

- **Munich malt:** Kilned higher still, but retains enough enzymes to convert itself. It lends a pale amber color and wonderful bready quality.

Color Malts

Color malts undergo further kilning and steeping to create a range of colors and flavors. Higher kilning temperatures cause Maillard reactions from the interaction of malt proteins and sugars with heat. Variables like the amount and type of proteins and sugars, moisture content, pH, and temperature, all have a big effect on the flavor, aroma, and colors produced. Colored malts are used to add depth,

Barley Varieties

Many base malts are labeled with the name of their barley variety —e.g., Maris Otter, Golden Promise, Barke, Chevallier. These can be modern or heirloom barleys, and since properties like protein content, which affect the finished beer, can be variety-dependent, the differences between malts (and beers) produced from different barley varieties can be striking.

complexity, and yes, color. But because the extra processing alters or destroys enzymes and other constituents of the source grain, they must be used in conjunction with a base malt and can only compose a fraction of the grist. Color malts include:

- **Caramel & crystal malt:** Produced by "mashing" germinated malt in the husk prior to kilning. This yields some complex sugars which will remain after fermentation, contributing body and sweetness. The temperature and extent of kilning can yield a wide range of colors from light to dark, and flavors from pastry to dark fruit. These malts are often designated by their Lovibond (°L) rating, with higher numbers indicating darker color.

- **Toasted/high-kilned malt:** Higher temps in kilning result in darker colors than base malt, with more biscuit and intensified bready flavors. Examples include amber, biscuit, and brown malts.

- **Roasted malt:** These are kilned at still higher temperatures, resulting in colors from deep garnet to black and flavors of coffee, chocolate, and cocoa. Examples include chocolate, black, Carafa, and Perla Negra.

Other Grains

Barley is unquestionably fantastic, but there's a whole world of other grains out there. A few notables:

- **Wheat malt:** Gives a wonderful fluffy texture and tart, doughy flavor.

- **Rye malt:** Enhances mouthfeel and foam and adds a spicy, minty, earthy flavor.

- **Oat malt:** Gives a silky texture and improved foam stability, with a low-key grainy flavor.

- **Spelt malt:** This heirloom wheat has a bit higher protein than modern wheat, so it does great things for body and foam.

HOPS

Brewers have been using plants to flavor beer since at least the Middle Ages, but probably for much longer. Historically, this included a wide range of herbs, spices, flowers, roots, assorted tree parts, and myriad other botanicals, depending on local availability as well as tradition, folklore, and secret family recipe.

Hops (*Humulus lupulus*) started out as just one of the many items used to flavor beer. It is a flowering climbing plant native to Europe, Asia, and North and South America. It belongs to the family *Cannabaceae*, along with the cannabis plant, and contains some of the same compounds as that species.

By late in the preindustrial era, hops had become the predominant beer flavoring in much of Europe. In our current craft beer renaissance, hops have grown from a mere flavoring agent, to an organoleptic centerpiece and marketing focal point. Many hop-forward styles highlight a variety—Centennial, Citra, Galaxy, and so forth—in the same way a wine might be called by its constituent grape.

HOP AGRONOMY

Hops are dioecious, meaning that a plant is either male or female. The part used by brewers is the flower of the female plant, so every hop bine you see climbing a trellis in a hopyard is female. And because seeds would take up energy from the female plant that would otherwise be devoted to producing desirable acids and oils, male plants are removed to prevent pollination.

Hops grow best in the temperate latitudes of both hemispheres— between 35° and 55° north or south. Major hop-producing countries include Germany, the United States, China, the Czech Republic, and Poland. France, Slovenia, England, Australia, and New Zealand don't produce hops at the same volume as the former countries, but their crops are nonetheless well-known to brewers worldwide for their distinctive varieties.

In an April 2017 presentation, Historian Ron Pattinson remarked that "everything revolutionary in brewing today is being done by hop farmers; brewers themselves aren't doing anything new, and brewers from hundreds of years ago were already doing much weirder shit than anyone is today."

HOP REGIONS WE HAVE KNOWN & LOVED

(in no particular order)

- **Yakima Valley, Washington State.** The rain shadow of the Cascade Mountains is the beating heart of American hop farming, producing more than 70% of the annual US crop. *You know it for: Cascade, CTZ, Simcoe, Amarillo, El Dorado, the list goes on.*

- **Hallertau, Bavaria, Germany.** The single largest hop-growing region in the world, home to more than 1,300 farms which produce more than 20 percent of the world's hop crop. *You know it for: Hallertau Mittelfrüh, Hersbrucker.*

- **Tettnang, Baden-Wurttemburg, Germany.** They've only been growing hops here for 1,000 years, and they have an eponymous landrace hop, no big deal. *You know it for: Tettnang.*

- **Nelson, New Zealand.** In the 19th century, immigrants from England and Germany tried planting hops on the sheltered coast of New Zealand's South Island, and the hops really liked it there. The New Zealand Hop Research Centre was founded in Nelson province in the 1950s and gave the world its first triploid hop plants. *You know it for: Nelson Sauvin, Wakatu, Rakau, Moutere, Motueka, and every other variety with a Maori name.*

- **Žatec, Czech Republic.** Like Tettnang, hop farming in this region near the German border dates back a millennium and can take at least partial credit for the miracle that is Czech Pilsner. *You know it for: Saaz.*

- **Kent, England.** Situated in southeast England between London and the English Channel, Kent was the beachhead for the invasion of hopped beer from the continent that eventually did away with the tradition of gruit on the sceptered isle.
  You know it for: East Kent Golding, Fuggle, Challenger, Target, Northdown, First Gold.

HOP FORMATS

Brewing scientist and author Charlie Bamforth observes that "The hop is remarkable among agricultural products in that essentially its sole outlet is for brewing."

Hops in beer used to mean the cone or flower, but eventually came to include the familiar pellets made from milled and pressed hop cones. Pellets store better than cones—their lower surface-to-volume ratio does a better job of protecting the delicate hop oils and acids from deterioration due to light, heat, and oxygen. They're also easier to dose into beer and dispose of. Whole cones still have their adherents among pro and hobby brewers, and some make it a point of pride to use "whole hops." In recent years, hop suppliers have been working on new formats, and now CO_2-derived hop extracts and resins and pure lupulin powders are becoming available to homebrewers. It's an exciting time to be a hophead.

USING HOPS

When exposed to the sustained high heat of boiling wort, the resinous acids in the hop flower are isomerized into bitter-tasting compounds that are a perfect counterpoint to the grainy, bready sweetness of malt. A significant fringe benefit, and one that was not lost on brewers of yore, is that these same hop acids have preservative and antimicrobial properties, improving the quality and shelf stability (and foam stability!) of beer.

Another reason brewers continue to use hops is because they're delicious. Those same tiny resin-containing glands sheltered by the petal-like bracts of the hop cone also house a spectrum of aromatic oils. These delicate oils are lost through volatilization over the course of a full boil, but when added near the end of the boil—or even on the cold side of the brewing process—they are released into wort or beer to contribute an array of aromas and flavors, hence those descriptors on beer menus of "pine," "grapefruit," and "watermelon Jolly Rancher."

ESSENTIAL HOP OILS

Essential oils comprise well under three percent of a hop cone's weight, but supply all of its inviting sensory qualities. The exact composition of oils depends on hop variety, and brewing chemists have identified hundreds of different oils in the hop. Here are a few of the major ones you'll encounter:

Caryophyllene	Black pepper, spicy
Farnesene	Floral
Geraniol	Floral, rose
Humulene	Earthy, woodsy, herbal
Myrcene	Floral, herbal, fruity
Limonene	Citrus
Linalool	Floral, citrus

WAYS HOPS ARE USED IN THE BREWHOUSE (AND IN THE RECIPES IN THIS BOOK)

Hot side

- **Mash hopping** is adding hops (usually whole cone) to the mash tun along with the grist. Because the hops are separated from the wort along with the spent grain, they are never exposed to boiling temperatures and do not yield much bitterness. Though mash hopping can result in some level of flavor similar to first wort hopping (below.) This technique is mainly used for either very low-bitterness beers like Berliner weisse, or very high-bitterness beers like double IPA.

- **First wort hopping** is adding a dose of bittering hops to wort in the boil kettle before the boil actually begins, and they remain in the kettle for the entire duration of the boil. The initial wort collected from the lauter tun is relatively high in pH, which makes flavor-active hop compounds more soluble and stable, resulting in heightened hop flavor in the finished beer. And because the temperature of the runoff wort is high enough to effect some isomerization, it results in a bit more bitterness than if the same amount of hops were added at the very beginning of the boil. FWH can be used in just about any recipe, but will yield the best results in ales or lagers where we want a subtle, refined hop character—heaps of late hops or dry hops will only eclipse any effect you achieve here.

- **Boil additions** are where the vast majority of a beer's hop bitterness is created. The higher the alpha acid content of a hop, and the longer the duration it's boiled for, the higher the bitterness yielded in the finished beer. Hops added late in the boil will yield less bitterness, but more of their flavor and aroma will remain in the finished beer. Boil additions are fundamental to pretty much every Western beer style of the modern era.

- **Whirlpool, hop back, or hop stand additions** are made while the wort is no longer at a boil but still hot enough to effect some isomerization of the bitter acids. In a commercial brewhouse, this process might be conducted in a whirlpool vessel or a small insert, called a hop back, in the line that carries the hot wort to the fermentor. For many homebrewers, it happens in the boil kettle itself—a strategy called a hop stand—in which the flame is killed, but the hops are left to steep before the wort is chilled. By extracting those wonderful volatile oils with very little bitterness, hop stands are great for styles that demand the maximum presence of fruity, piney hop aromatics.

Cold side

- **Dry hopping** is the addition of hops to beer in the fermentor or conditioning vessel to amplify hop flavor. Traditionally, dry hopping takes place after primary fermentation is complete. But brewers of hazy IPAs have been pushing it further up in the process, adding dry hops to primary with the understanding that hop compounds are biotransformed into other ethereal flavors and aromas during active fermentation. Dry hopping is practically synonymous with IPA and other highly hop-forward beers.

- **Cask hopping** is thought to have originated with ale brewers in England. They added dry hops to the cask, which served as both shipping and serving vessel, primarily for their preservative qualities, where they would have helped inhibit souring bacteria. A secondary benefit is a terrific, fresh flavor and aroma imparted to the beer during maturation. This technique is awesome for English bitters and pale ales as well as their American cousins. *Nota bene*: Whole cone flowers can be sunk in a cask or keg in a sanitized mesh bag and won't clog lines or hand-pumps like pellets will.

- **Inline infusions**, also colloquially known as "Randalls," are achieved by means of a filter situated inline between a keg and the tap which is packed with whole cone hops. Beer is pushed through the filter full of hops en route to the glass, picking up flavor and aroma on the way. And of course, just about anything could be put in there alongside or instead of hops, like fruit, cacao nibs, whole spices, or Girl Scout cookies.

YEAST

It was mysterious and intangible when brewing first began. We knew that some external force was at work in the wort, and explanations tended towards the mystical. But even before we discovered the true nature of yeast, we knew that beer is impossible without it.

Barley, wheat, rye, hop cones and hop pellets all have immediately tangible, readily identifiable qualities. Brewers work with them more or less manually. You can inspect a jar of these raw materials on a brewery tour and instantly get a good idea of how they contribute to your beer.

Yeast, on the other hand, works alone and in the dark. It's microscopic; you can't really show it off to a tour group, and you can't hold a flask full of slurry and have the same intuitive understanding of what it will do for the finished product.

If beer were a car, malt would be the frame, wheels, and gas tank; hops would be the rims, spoiler, and airbrushed dragons. But yeast is the engine and, since that's how we get anywhere, it's worth learning a bit more about what it is.

WHAT IS YEAST?

Yeast is a single-celled eukaryotic (all genetic material contained in the nucleus) fungus, and it's a damn life-affirming everyday miracle because it turns sugar into alcohol. Some anthropologists hypothesize that brewing beer was the reason ancient humans transitioned from hunter/gatherer to agrarian societies, paving the way for civilization itself—which would put the domestication of yeast right up there with the discovery of fire, wheels, and Led Zeppelin.

When introduced to a food source like beer wort, yeast cells transfer sugar molecules across their cell walls and, through a series of complex metabolic pathways, break them down for energy and create ethanol and CO_2 gas as byproducts. Yeast doesn't care at all about your beer, it's just trying to survive. Cells reproduce by budding—daughter cells form on the wall of a mother cell, receiving a portion of the nucleus before splitting off and starting the life cycle anew.

Yeast is omnipresent, and can be found on plants, animals, porous surfaces—even, as Rogue Brewing famously demonstrated a few years ago, in their founder's beard. Before its life cycle could be observed and understood, its introduction into beer wort would have been accidental, or at least incidental.

A HISTORY OF YEAST IN THREE PARAGRAPHS

Prior to the modern age and microscopy, yeast was not recognized as a living organism but its action was certainly observable. The word fermentation is rooted in the Latin "fevere" (to boil), which, if you've ever been to a brewery and seen a big conical venting into a bucket of water, you'll agree is an apt description.

Dark ages brewers called the mysterious transformative agent "godisgood" and quasi-magical "barm sticks" were transferred from batch to batch. Unbeknownst to the brewers, the wood itself (of the brewing vessels as well as the barm sticks) actually housed colonies of yeast, inoculating the fresh wort that came into contact with them. Over time, these populations of yeast would have selectively mutated to adapt to their specialized environment—gradually developing tolerance to a certain temperatures and alcohol levels, passing along desirable sedimenting habits, and other behaviors we value and expect from our brewing yeast today.

In the Middle Ages, yeast cells were first observed but not understood—alchemists believed that ethanol was already present but had to be separated from "impurities" like yeast and CO_2. That theory held sway for hundreds of years, until the 19th century when microbiology was established as a science and proved that yeast was the agent of fermentation, not a byproduct.

UN POQUITO LATIN

There are two great families of beer: ale and lager, with membership determined by the type of yeast used in its fermentation.

Saccharomyces cerevisiae is sometimes used as a blanket term or general synonym for "brewing yeast," but it properly and specifically refers to ale yeast. *S. cerevisiae* encompasses a vast range of characteristics—everything from the clean and crisp (Sierra Nevada's "Chico," and German Kölsch) to buttery and fruity (English) to phenolic and funky (hefeweizen, Belgian).

Unlike lager yeast, ale strains do not seem to share a recent common origin or similar genetic fingerprints. They will happily ferment and grow at temperatures up to 98°F or above, but slow significantly or go dormant below about 50°F.

Lager yeast belongs to *Saccharomyces pastorianus*, a more recent hybrid of *S. cerevisiae* and *S. eubayanus*. It only shares 60 percent of its genome with *S. cerevisiae* and seems to have inherited its cold tolerance from *S. eubayanus*—it can continue to ferment and reproduce at temperatures that would send *S. cerevisiae* into dormancy.

Genome sequencing has shown that lager yeasts originated from one or two common sources, which makes any two strains of *S. pastorianus* more closely related than any two strains of *S. cerevisiae* are to one another.

What Is A Strain?

We often hear brewers refer to different types of *S. cerevisiae* or *S. pastorianus* as a "strain" of yeast. A yeast strain would be defined by a microbiologist as a genetic isolate that can be distinguished from other isolates of the same species by DNA variations that express themselves through different, specific characteristics.

What this means for brewers is that these characteristics—flavors, aromas, and behavior like flocculation or alcohol tolerance, which are passed from mother cell to daughter cell—can be replicated from batch to batch, allowing for predictable fermentations and consistent beer.

CREATOR OF FLAVOR

It's difficult to understate the importance of yeast to the finished beer we pour into our glasses. This little fungus can generate over 500 flavor-active compounds during fermentation, and the vast majority of beer aromas and flavors we experience are at least affected, if not created, by yeast.

In their mission to survive by glycolysis, the cells produce more than just ethanol and CO_2. A small percentage of their output is a range of flavor-active compounds—esters, phenols, diacetyl, fusels, aldehydes, and more. How perceptible these byproducts are depends greatly on a brewer's choice of strain and the environment into which it's introduced. Whether they're desireable or defective is greatly dependent on the beer style and the drinker.

There is both nature and nurture at play. Yeast strains like those for Belgian saison or Bavarian hefeweizen have a gene which triggers production of phenolic compounds as part of their metabolic process, which gives those beers their signature spicy, peppery character. In lager strains, this gene is set to "off," and so their fermentations will lack those phenolic compounds.

But being a sensitive living organism, the yeast's environment will affect its fermentation byproducts. Warm fermentation causes rapid growth, which leads to higher ester production, while excess oxygen can cause higher levels of fusels.

Today, many beers are filtered or at least fined to separate yeast, so that we're just tasting what they've left behind. Unfiltered cask ales or bottle-conditioned beers are "live" products, with further flavor development fostered by the yeast that's still in contact with, and working on, the packaged beer. An extreme example are weissebiers or some Belgian ales, where sedimented yeast is roused and reintro-duced, to create a cloudy appearance and nutty, bready flavor.

Tens of trillions of yeast cells likely went into the tank that pro-duced the beer I hope you're enjoying right now, so let's pour a little out for all our microscopic homies.

CARE & FEEDING, AND OTHER PRACTICAL CONSIDERATIONS

So you got some yeast cells ... now what?

Formats

Yeast strains for homebrewers are available as either liquid or dried cultures.

Liquid yeast is sold as an aseptically-packaged slurry. It's highly perishable and temperature-sensitive, so it should be stored below 40°F and used within a few months of purchase at most. There are multiple labs producing liquid yeast cultures for homebrewers, and one of its biggest advantages is the number of options—there are many more, and more specialized, strains available in liquid format, particularly for Brett and sour beer brewing.

Dried brewers yeast will look familiar if you've ever baked your own bread before. It looks like baking yeast, housed in a foil sachet as a granular powder. These dehydrated yeast cells can be reconstituted in warm water to create a slurry for inoculating wort. Because the process of dehydrating yeast is equipment-intensive, there are not many labs producing dried brewers yeast, and the selection of strains is not as great as it is in liquid. The tradeoff is a much more shelf-stable and less perishable product, which won't lose viability if unrefrigerated as quickly as liquid yeast, and with a best-before date that's years instead of months after packaging.

How to choose

By the time their cultures go into a pack, vial, or sachet, yeast labs have already done a lot of legwork for both hobby and pro brewer. Their websites, literature, and even product names can quickly help you narrow down the right strain for your recipe: German Ale for a Kölsch, ESB for a bitter, Oktoberfest for an Oktoberfest.

Which isn't to say you can't go off-piste and select a strain based on matching its parameters to your desired outcome:

- **Temperature range** has a big influence not only on the yeast's production of flavor-active compounds (or lack thereof), but also on it generally behaving the way it's supposed to. Match a strain based on the temperature at which you're able to let it ferment: if your fermentation area is hovering around 58°F, don't choose a strain with a range of 65°-75°F unless you can supply some heat. Likewise, if a strain does best if the ferment is kept between 45° and 56°F, don't expect it to perform as described if it never got cooler than 70°F.

- **Attenuation** is a measurement of how much of the available wort sugars are converted by the yeast during fermentation. A higher-attenuating yeast strain will make for a drier-tasting beer with lower final gravity and more alcohol, while a lower-attenuating strain will do the opposite—sweeter finish, higher final gravity and less alcohol. Match the strain to the desired profile of the finished beer.

- **Flocculation** is the tendency of yeast cells to adhere to one another as fermentation winds down, forming visible (sometimes large) clumps which then settle to the bottom of the fermentor, leaving the young beer bright, with less haze. There's usually an inverse relationship between attenuation and flocculation. Because highly flocculent strains can't keep fermenting once they've dropped to the bottom of the tank, they also tend to have lower attenuation and make for a full-bodied beer. Because they allow for a pretty clear beer quickly and with minimal intervention, they are good candidates for beers that need to be packaged and served fresh.

"Powdery" strains with low flocculation keep fermenting since they stay in suspension longer, typically yielding a drier beer with lower final gravity and more alcohol. However, this also means the beer will probably remain hazy after primary fermentation concludes, requiring more time and/or fining agents to drop clear.

- **Alcohol tolerance** usually isn't a concern most beer styles. Given good cell health and favorable environmental conditions in the carboy or bucket, any strain of brewers *Saccharomyces* should be able to handle up to 8-10 percent ABV. But for very strong beers like Scotch ales, Belgian quads, or barleywines, it can start to be a concern. When the expected alcohol content of your post-fermentation beer creeps into the double digits, look for strains that can handle it.

On brew day

You've chosen your yeast strain, stored it cold, and now it's time to make it some dinner in the form of wort.

Depending on yeast format, the lab's instructions, and the recipe, it may be anywhere from a good idea to mandatory to propagate the yeast in a starter to make sure there's a sufficient population to make that wort into tasty, tasty beer. The recipes in this book note when and where a yeast starter is appropriate (which is almost always.) Please see the **Brewday Walkthrough** section for steps on propagating yeast in a starter culture.

WATER

Roughly 95 percent of beer is water. It impacts every part of brewing, from the chemistry of the mash, to performance of the yeast cells during fermentation, all the way through to the flavor of the final product in the glass. For all the attention lavished on malt, hops, and yeast, water is truly the unsung member of the beer quadrumvirate.

Water is more than just what's in our pint—brewing is an extremely water-intensive process. Beyond being used as a raw material during mashing and sparging, brewers rely on water for cleaning and sanitizing as well as temperature control and chilling. Every gallon of beer requires many times that volume in water to produce.

WATER FOR BREWING

To be suitable for use in brewing, water has to meet some of the same basic criteria as any drinking water: It has to be potable, free of contaminants and pathogens, and free of unpleasant aromas or flavors.

For many homebrewers today, that's as complex as you need to make it, if you so choose. But for the professional brewer, it may be a beer's most complicated component.

A deep dive (pardon me) into water chemistry is outside the scope of this book. But let's at least take a quick dip.

Mineral content and hardness

The water we get from our faucets picks up minerals and trace elements from the rocks and sand in the aquifers through which it travels to our wells. Because the geology of these aquifers can be very different depending on where you are, the water that comes from them can also be very different, and lend distinct qualities to the beers which they are used to brew.

Regional differences in water helped shape many of the world's great beer styles—the extremely soft water of Pilsen is integral to the softly hoppy and elegant Bohemian Pilsner style; the hard and mineral-rich waters of Burton-on-Trent and Dortmund lent themselves to producing sharply bitter ales and lagers; and the carbonate-rich waters of Dublin and Munich were ideal for brewing dark beers like stout and dunkel.

A note on water hardness

We just referenced the "soft" water of Pilsen and the "hard" waters of Dortmund: Hardness is a concept used to describe the calcium and magnesium content of water, as expressed in mg/L or ppm. A water with 0 to 60 mg/L (as calcium carbonate) would be considered soft; 61 to 120 mg/L would be moderately hard; 121 to 180 mg/L is hard; and more than 180 mg/L would be classified as very hard water.

Some usual suspects you'll see on water reports, and what they mean for brewing:

Compound	What It Does
Calcium (Ca)	Decreases mash pH, improves hot break, stabilizes amylase enzymes, enhances extraction of hop bitterness, aids yeast flocculation. High levels can inhibit uptake of Mg by yeast cells.
Magnesium (Mg)	Cofactor in yeast metabolism; enhances flavor, decreases mash pH. Excessive amounts can result in unpleasant flavors in the beer (and a laxative effect on the drinker).
Carbonate (CO_3)	Enhances malt flavor, strong alkaline buffer against pH change, reduces tannins. High levels create harsh bitterness.
Sulfate (SO_4)	Enhances bitterness and dryness, increases mash pH. Can be a source for H_2S gas created during fermentation.
Chloride (Cl)	Enhances bitterness and mouthfeel, improves clarity. High levels can be toxic to yeast.

pH

pH is a scale used to measure how acidic or basic a substance is. It's expressed on a scale from 0 (acidic) to 14 (basic), with 7 being neutral.

For our purposes, pH plays a large role in the chemistry of the mash and in the stability of the finished beer. A pH that's out of spec can impede enzymatic action in mash and protein coagulation in the boil, or lead to unpleasant bitterness from hop additions and leave the finished beer more susceptible to infection.

The pH of brewing water can be manipulated up or down through acid and salt additions, or by blending water with a different pH value to make sure it's copacetic for brewing processes. pH is also affected by the malts used in the mash and the fermentation itself, so if you're interested in the minutiae of beer or in refining your process, invest in some pH test strips or a digital pH meter to help monitor.

Process Stage	Optimum pH
Mash	5.1-5.3 ideal, but enzymes active from 5.0-5.7
Boil	Same as for mash
Post-fermentation (standard beers)	4.0-4.7, depending on yeast, other ingredients, and process
Post-fermentation (sour beers)	3.2-4.0, depending on yeast & bacteria strains, ingredients, and process

Alkalinity

"Alkalinity is arguably the most important parameter to the brewer," write Kaminski and Palmer, "because it has the biggest effect on mash performance."

The alkalinity of water is a measure of its buffering capacity—its resistance to changes in pH. Alkalinity is determined by carbonate content; the higher the amount of $CaCO_3$ in the water report, the less it will want to allow pH to drop, which can be problematic for the mash if we're using high-pH water.

Highly alkaline water can be treated with the addition of food-safe acid (phosphoric or lactic acid should be readily available at your LHBS) or acidifying calcium salts.

THEORY INTO PRACTICE

Besides being the most abundant component of beer, water is argu-ably also its most complicated. Manipulation of pH and mineral content can become complex pretty quickly, and regional and sea-sonal variances in water sources, different target water profiles for different beers (remember the soft water for Pils and hard water for IPA?) and different desired outcomes make a one-size-fits all water treatment solution very difficult if not impossible.

Whether you choose to circumvent this entirely by buying reverse-osmosis water as a "blank slate" and build a water profile to spec through salt additions, or to treat the water you have, brewing software programs and online calculators are an immense help.

Further reading:

- *Water: A Comprehensive Guide for Brewers* by Palmer and Kaminski
- *A Textbook of Brewing Vol. 1* by Jean DeClerck

BREWDAY WALKTHROUGH

These steps are general guidelines and assume you're already familiar with the all-grain brewing process—refer to the instructions for your brew system, and adjust as needed based on experience with your own particular equipment.

Except where noted, the recipes in this book are formulated for 5 gallon (19 liter) all-grain batches, calculated at 75 percent mash efficiency.

At home, I use the old-fashioned fly sparge technique, which makes me a get-off-my-lawn-grade Luddite. Brewers who batch sparge, or who conduct BIAB (brew-in-a-bag) or other no-sparge mash regimens, or who use automated systems, will need to calculate water volumes based on their process and systems.

PREPARATIONS

1. **APPROXIMATELY 1 DAY BEFORE: Propagate yeast.** When using liquid yeast, these recipes will yield the best results if we make a yeast starter 24-36 hours prior to brew day—the exceptions are very low-gravity ales, where the pitch rate right out of the pack is usually sufficient for a 5 gallon batch.

2. **DAY OF: Collect mash water.** On my system, I use approximately 1.3 quarts per pound. Adjust as needed for your process and system.

3. **DAY OF: Mill the grains.** If you didn't already have this done for you at the shop, now's the time.

Preparing A Yeast Starter

The best substrate for propagating beer yeast is beer wort. For starter cultures, an all-malt wort of 1.040 OG, plus a bit of supplemental nutrient, is ideal. Get a pound or three of light dry malt extract for starters from your LHBS—it's easy to find, easy to measure, and easy to store the leftovers for future use.

Equipment

- Sanitized Erlenmeyer flask or mason jar, 2 liters capacity
- Sanitized cover for the flask or jar—this could be a square of aluminum foil, a foam stopper, or a loose-fitting lid
- Oven mitts or hot pads (bonus points for floral pattern)
- Magnetic stir plate and bar (optional, but very beneficial)

Basic Recipe (scale as needed)

- 3.5 ounces (100 grams) plain dry malt extract (approximately ½ cup)
- ½ teaspoon yeast nutrient
- 1 quart (1L) H_2O

Basic Procedure

- **Mix DME, nutrient, and water.** Shake or stir to dissolve as much as possible.
- **Boil the starter wort.** Use a saucepan on a kitchen stove; if using a

MASH & SPARGE

1. **Add all grains** to strike water and mix to achieve the temperature specified in the recipe. It should be as uniform as possible, with no dough balls (unmixed clumps of milled grain that are dry at the center) or hot spots. Rest the mash at this temperature for approximately 60 minutes, give or take; or until conversion is complete.

2. **While the mash rests,** collect and heat sparge water (if used in your process.)

3. **When the mash rest (or rests) are complete,** heat the mash to 170°F for mashout—this will denature the enzymes, stabilizing the fermentability of the wort, and expediting sugar extraction

laboratory-grade glass flask, you may be able to boil directly in the flask—doublecheck with your supplier or the manufacturer first.

- **Cool to 70°F using a cold-water bath.** Whether cooling in a saucepan or flask, keep it covered to maintain sanitary conditions.

- **Transfer cooled wort to sanitized flask or jar.** Pour the cooled starter wort into the sanitized flask or jar.

- **Add yeast pack.** Cover loosely with sanitized aluminum foil, a foam stopper, or the jar's lid and swirl gently to mix.

- **Incubate 24-36 hours at 70°F.** Whether lager or ale, cells reproduce faster at warm temps—at this point, we're just out to make more yeast, not beer, so don't worry about temperature-related flavors in the starter. Agitate the flask or jar periodically, or—better yet—use a stir plate to keep cells in suspension and supplied with a steady trickle of oxygen.

- **A note on timing:** Cell growth is typically maximized within 24-36 hours, and, because of the high cell density in a starter culture, extending this time can be counterproductive and result in a decrease in the yeast population. If for some reason you can't use the starter within ~36 hours, it's best to store it in the fridge for approximately 1 week.

- **Pitch into main batch.** Pour the starter culture into the cooled, aerated wort in your fermentor; the entire volume of starter may be added to the main batch, or you may prefer to decant some of the spent wort first: chill the starter during brew day to encourage cells to settle, then decant the top layer into the sink, pouring just the yeasty bottom layer into the fermentor.

when the wort is separated from the spent mash solids.

4. **Sparge and collect the wort in the boil kettle**—however you do, be it false bottom or manifold or mesh bag or gravity or robot.

BOIL

- **Boil the wort for at least 60 minutes,** with hops and other ingredients added as specified. Addition times are referred to with T-minus numbers, indicating the number of minutes from the end of the boil (the beginning of the boil is T-60, the end is T-0.) If the recipe requires a hopstand or steeping period after the boil, the count will go positive (e.g. cool the wort at T+20.)

- **Once the wort is boiled,** cool it as quickly as possible. Aim to match the fermentation temperature specified in the recipe, or—ideally—even a few degrees cooler.

- **Transfer the cooled wort** to a sanitized fermentor, making sure the wort is well aerated and oxygenated.

FERMENTATION AND CONDITIONING

1. **Pitch yeast and seal fermentor.** We could also call this "inoculation," which sounds even more sciencey. Pour the starter (or, if you didn't make a starter, pour the yeast direct from the pack or vial) directly into the wort. Seal the fermentor and attach an airlock.

2. **Fermentation.** How long this takes depends greatly on environmental factors—temperature, oxygen, wort composition and gravity, and the yeast strain itself. Generally, ale fermentations should be complete within about one week, lagers closer to two weeks—but warmer temperatures, lower wort gravities, and higher O_2 levels and pitch rates will all make things go faster, so hard timelines are kinda useless. Use a hydrometer and listen to your beer.

3. **When fermentation subsides and gravity is stable,** the recipe may call for racking to a secondary fermentor, and further additions, like dry hops or additional yeast; or it may proceed directly to packaging. Refer to individual recipes for specifics.

PACKAGING

When fermentation is complete, any post-fermentation additions have been made, and flavor and clarity are to your liking, it's time to package and carbonate the bright beer. Refer to the instructions that came with your equipment for specifics on bottle priming or kegging.

FINAL STEP

Drink it like you brewed it.

Quick And Dirty Lagering

I love brewing lagers—the traditions and arcana of the process, the fussiness of the fermentation, the purity of malt and hop flavors that result. They're time- and energy-intensive though, for pro as well as homebrewers: traditional lager fermentation regimens require weeks—if not months—of bulk storage at low temperatures after primary fermentation and before packaging.

Recently, though, American brewers have been experimenting with an abbreviated lager schedule that can shave weeks—if not months—off the production cycle. By circumventing the formation of esters with a cold start, but promoting rapid reduction of diacetyl with a warm finish—all during primary fermentation—the yeast's work is finished and only thing left to do is crash-cool for clarification, which can be complete in as little as a week or two.

Here's an outline of how to implement this in your home brewery:

- **Aerate well.** Too little dissolved oxygen can lead to higher sulfur production during fermentation, which will not taste delicious four weeks from now when we want to be packaging this beer.

- **Pitch cold.** Add yeast when the wort temp is approximately 45-48°F—this will suppress ester formation without shutting down yeast metabolism entirely.

- **Increase temp as fermentation progresses.** Once fermentation is well underway, begin gradually increasing the ferment temperature, in small daily increments, up to approximately 58°F. Besides speeding up the reuptake of diacetyl by the yeast as well as the last bit of attenuation, SO_2 and other compounds will be offgassed more readily.

- **Crash cool.** When gravity is stable and diacetyl is below the taste perception threshold ("VDK negative," in the parlance of our times), drop the temperature to 33-37°F for clarification. Whereas this portion of the traditional lagering phase would last several weeks or more, in this regimen the beer can be ready to package in under two weeks.

Illustration by David Witt

NECK TAT THAT SAYS "EVIL" BLACK IPA

Targets: **OG:** 1.075, **IBU:** 65–70, **SRM:** 27, **ABV:** 8.0%

At a recent brewing conference, I sat next to a guy with a neck tattoo that was simply the word "evil."

At least I think that's what it said—I was too scared to stare directly and it was hard to read the stylized script with a semi-averted gaze. Even if that wasn't what his tattoo actually said, or if the guy didn't actually have a neck tat and just badly missed his mouth with some heavily sauced brisket, well, as the man said, never let the truth get in the way of a good story.

But at that same conference, I had the chance to try an award-winning American black ale—more than once—and it was very good. Both of these experiences left an impression that are now converging in this recipe.

Some may know it as black IPA, or Cascadian dark ale, or bullshit hoppy porter, or some other adjective-laden and possibly contradictory term. The Brewers Association calls it American-style black ale. But whatever the name, it should be stout- or porter-like in color, hoppy in aroma and flavor, but not astringent or acidic in its roast.

We're going to aim at the upper limits of the style for gravity, bitterness, and ABV percentage. We'll get some classic Pacific Northwest IPA hops and make sure they cannot be overlooked in the glass through heavy additions late in the boil and a hopstand prior to cooling. To get deep, dark color without astringency or bitterness, we'll use a de-husked roast grain combined with a separate cold steeping process. In both neck tats and American black ales, subtlety is for losers.

SHOPPING LIST

- 12.5 lbs. Rahr Pale Ale
- 1 lb. Patagonia Perla Negra (bagged separately)

- 0.5 oz. Chinook
- 2 oz. Simcoe
- 2 oz. Centennial
- 2 oz. Amarillo

- Wyeast 1056 American Ale

- Mesh bag for cold-steeping the Perla Negra.

KEY POINTS FOR KEY PINTS

Yeast starter: Diacetyl, esters, incomplete fermentation—the side effects of stressed yeast cells are not metal, so make a starter the day before.

Cold steeping: The Perla Negra should be cold-steeped for 24 hours prior to brew day—this is just like brewing cold press coffee—then strained. The resulting inky liquid is added to the kettle during the last few minutes of the boil for an intense, chocolate-and-coffee roast malt character and deep color with minimal harshness.

Hopstanding: Most of the hops in this recipe don't go in until the last 10 minutes of the boil, or until after the boil is shutdown. About 66% of the IBU are from about 85% of the hops—not exactly a picture of efficient use. Along with bitterness, hopstanding brings a big dose of fragrant hop oils and resin, which would otherwise be lost in a rolling boil.

BREWING

PREP *(24 hours prior)*
- Make a yeast starter. Then mill the Perla Negra, place in a mesh bag, and soak in 2–3 quarts of cold or room-temp brewing water.

PREP *(brew day)*
- Mill the base malt, then collect and heat strike water to about 165°F.

MASH & SPARGE
- **Mash rest:** Add base malt to strike water, mix to 151–153°F, and rest for 60–90 minutes. Collect and heat sparge water.
- **Mashout:** Heat to 170°F for 5 minutes.
- Sparge and collect the wort in the boil kettle.

BOIL *(60 minutes)*
- **T-60:** 0.5 oz. Chinook. Then remove the bag of Perla Negra from the steeping liquid—use a colander to let it drain and collect the liquid. Discard the grain.
- **T-10:** 1 oz. each Centennial, Simcoe, and Amarillo, and the reserved cold steeping liquid.
- **T-0:** Turn off the burner. Add 1 oz. each Centennial, Simcoe, and Amarillo. Let steep.
- **T+20:** Cool the wort, transfer to sanitized fermentor, aerate well, and pitch yeast.

FERMENTATION AND BEYOND
- **Primary fermentation:** 8–10 days for the wort to reach terminal gravity. Aim for 65°F.
- If you can, cool the finished beer to encourage the yeast to drop and allow another week or two to condition and then package. Enjoy this one fresh.

1997 IPA

Targets: **OG:** 1.057, **IBU:** 50–55, **SRM:** 9, **ABV:** 7%

<old man rant>
Some of us here can remember a time when craft beer—back then we called it "microbrew"—wasn't so complicated. It wasn't so fraught with issues of identity, craft versus "crafty," or the minefields of ownership and majority stakes. There were no paralyzing choices created by an entire wall of palate-erasing next-thing hop/acid show-pieces at the bottle shop. This was pre-IBU arms race. Pre-"dank." It was either a macro-industrial yella lager, or it wasn't.
</old man rant>

Not that I necessarily want to go back. I like "dank" just fine. And it's easier now than it has been for generations for Americans to get good, fresh beer "brewed in your town or the next town over," as Norman MacLean wrote. But nostalgia is a powerful thing and there's great appeal in simplicity.

In the "microbrew" era, IPA was not yet king. It was closer to what we would probably now pigeonhole as a 20th century English IPA. It was caramelly and deep in color because we were unencumbered by well-researched historical documents. It was citric and piney instead of cat-pissy and dank because Simcoe and Amarillo were not yet even a glimmer in a Yakima Valley breeding program's eye. We thought it was strong because 7 percent ABV was not yet entry-level.

Well, 1997 called and it wants its IPA back.

SHOPPING LIST

- 8.5 lbs. Rahr 2-Row
- 1 lb. Simpsons Crystal Medium or Patagonia Caramel 55L

- 12 oz. Weyermann Munich Malt
- 4 oz. Rahr Red Wheat Malt

- 1.75 oz. Chinook
- 1 oz. Willamette

- 2 oz. Cascade

- Wyeast 1056 American Ale

KEY POINTS FOR KEY PINTS

Chico = amigo: Can't miss with a classic. Good ol' 1056 is your friend for this formulation.

Alternative hop nation: Citra, Idaho 7, Azacca, El Dorado, Mosaic—any of your more recent hot-stuff hops would do just swimmingly in this recipe, but then it's going to taste like Pearl Jam is playing on the oldies station instead of the Top 40. Your call.

BREWING

PREP
- Make a yeast starter prior to brew day. Mill the grains. Heat strike water to 165°F.

MASH & SPARGE
- **Mash rest:** Add grains to strike water, mix to 151–153°F, and rest for 60–90 minutes. Collect and heat sparge water.
- **Mashout:** Heat to 170°F for 5 minutes.
- Sparge and collect the wort in the boil kettle.

BOIL *(60 minutes, while shaking your fist at the millennials on your lawn.)*
- **T-60:** 0.75 oz. Chinook.
- **T-15:** 0.5 oz. each Cascade and Chinook.
- **T-0:** 0.5 oz. each Cascade and Chinook.
- Cool the wort, transfer to a sanitized fermentor, aerate well, and pitch yeast.

FERMENTATION & BEYOND
- **Primary fermentation:** Aim for about 66–68°F. When fermentation activity begins to slow, allow the fermentor to warm up to approximately 70°F for a 2-3 day diacetyl rest.
- When the gravity is stable and the green beer is diacetyl-negative, rack to a sanitized secondary fermentor.
- Dry hop with 1 oz. each Cascade and Willamette. Rest with the dry hops for approximately five days, or until the hop flavor is to your liking. Fine as needed, then package and carbonate.
- Much like grunge, this IPA is best in the moment—don't let your kids rediscover it in twenty years.

LIQUID SWORDS THROWBACK IPA

Targets: **OG:** 1.060, **IBU:** 70+, **SRM:** 5, **ABV:** 6.2%

To know where you're going, you have to know where you've been; or, as the GZA puts it, sometimes you gotta take that shit back to the swords.

Thanks to an 1878 British military document, we know what specs the Raj wanted for a 19th century India pale ale: brewed November through May, 100 percent malt, OG over 1.060, a hopping rate of no less than 2–2.5 ounces per gallon (that's homebrew scale, and not including dry hops), casked "not more than 21 days after brewing," then aged for 9–12 months before bottling.

The beer would have been pale in color due to that newfangled 19th century pale ale malt, extremely bitter when fresh, less so with age, and probably quite clear and attenuated after a year in cask. Contrary to what you may have heard other MCs spit, those original IPAs were not necessarily high-alcohol—beer was a more temperate option than gin for colonists and officers, and brewers relied on the antibacterial qualities of hops to prolong its shelf life.

This won't taste like a modern IPA. The quality of English ale yeast, the hop varieties used, its sheer bitterness, and the lack of emphasis on "fresh hop" character speak to a different era and aesthetic. Some of these proto-IPAs were undrinkable when fresh, only becoming approachable after age had mellowed the hop quality. If you're feeling ambitious and historically accurate, double the amount of boil and dry hops, and taste it a year from now.

Extra credit: Burtonize it. For authenticity—and enhanced hop bitterness—match the mineral and ion content of your brewing water to that of Burton-on-Trent, England, a historical stronghold of English IPA. Use pre-blended "Burton Water Salts" (from your LHBS) or mix your own with food-grade calcium sulfate (gypsum) and magnesium sulfate (epsom salts.) Obtain a report on your water source (available on municipal websites) so you know the base levels of minerals and ions, brewing software to calculate the proper additions (I use BeerSmith), and a gram scale to weigh out the doses. Nerd up!

SHOPPING LIST

- 10.5 lbs. Crisp No. 19 Floor-Malted Maris Otter (or other high-quality UK pale ale malt)

- 5 oz. East Kent Golding

- A London-style or Burton-style yeast strain. I like Wyeast 1028 London Ale or WL023 Burton Ale.

KEY POINTS FOR KEY PINTS

One malt, one hop = no place to hide: Despite the intense flavor, this is still an elementally simple beer. The quality of the ingredients will show prominently in the finished product, so splashing out for primo base malt and doing due diligence on the crop year of the hops is well worth it.

Dry hop vs. cask/keg hop: Back when IPA was actually sent to India, the casks were dosed with a high rate of dry hops. This recipe calls for dry hopping in a secondary fermentor, but if you're a kegging homebrewer and want to get jiggy with cask/keg hops, just use a mesh bag and whole hops for the dry hop portion (pellets in a corny keg = clogged dip tubes.)

BREWING

PREP
- Make a yeast starter—we need a healthy population if we're going to get this into casks inside 21 days like the British military mandated.
- Mill the grains.
- Heat strike water to approximately 165°F.

MASH & SPARGE
- **Mash rest:** Add grains to strike water, mix to 151–153°F, and rest for 60–90 minutes. Collect and heat sparge water.
- **Mashout:** Heat to 170°F for 5 minutes.
- Sparge and collect the wort in the boil kettle.

BOIL *(90 minutes, while shining your monocle.)*
- **T-90:** 2.5 oz. East Kent Golding.
- **T-30:** 1.5 oz. East Kent Golding.
- **T-0:** Cool the wort, transfer to sanitized fermentor, aerate well, and pitch yeast.

FERMENTATION AND BEYOND
- **Primary fermentation:** Aim for around 65°F. When activity begins to slow, allow the fermentor to warm up to approximately 68–70°F for a 2–3 day diacetyl rest, about 7–10 days total.
- Rack to a secondary fermentor and add dry hops—use 1 oz. East Kent Golding (or a bit less if you plan to drink it sooner rather than later.)
- Condition the beer on the dry hops for at least a couple months. It will be quite aggressive while young—which may suit our 21st century craft beer sensibilities—but it will mellow and start showing nuances with more time under its belt.
- Serve at cellar temp (not fridge temp!) so as not to muffle the malt component of its profile, on a sweltering summer day alongside a big plate of vindaloo.

PEQUOD SESSION IPA

Targets: **OG:** 1.045, **IBU:** 43-45, **SRM:** 5.2, **ABV:** 4.6%

Say what you will about endless variations on an already ubiquitous style—this beer is an anti-whale. It doesn't age or travel particularly well. It's not for cellaring or note-taking or dissection. It's not for sniffing in your best crystal stemware. Simply put, this is a beer for drinking.

We get so hung up on the huge, elusive rarities in the beer world that we forget about beers brewed for simple enjoyment. Statistically speaking, it's what the vast majority of people, either now or historically, think of when they envision "having a beer." The pyramids were not built by workers fed on barrel-aged collaboration stouts. Welsh coal miners and Dortmunder steel workers were not camping out for rare beer releases.

Let's make an everyday beer for everyday people. Following in the tasty footsteps of Firestone Walker Easy Jack, Founders All Day, Ska Rudie, Lagunitas DayTime, and Oskar Blues Pinner, let's make a sub-five percent hop-juice crusher.

It is arguably Instagram-worthy, but then the entire time you're staging the pic, you're not enjoying the actual experience and the pint is hemorrhaging volatile hop terpenes, unappreciated, into the atmosphere.

#WhatAWaste

SHOPPING LIST

- 5.5 lbs. Rahr Pale Ale
- 1 lb. Rahr White Wheat malt
- 1 lb. Weyermann Munich I
- 12 oz. Simpsons Caramalt

- 1 oz. Idaho 7
- 1 oz. Galaxy
- 1 oz. Mandarina Bavaria

- Your favorite American or clean-ish English ale strain; I'm going to use Wyeast 1318 London Ale III.

KEY POINTS FOR KEY PINTS

Hop Selection: Mandarina Bavaria and Galaxy have been around for a minute, but Idaho 7 (citric/resiny experimental variety from—wait for it—Idaho) is a newbie to your LHBS. I really like the combination of pine-citrus with sweet tropical fruit from this specific blend; other good options would be Citra and/or Mosaic and/or Simcoe partnered with El Dorado and/or New Zealand Rakau.

Yeast selection: We don't want so many esters that the yeast character starts to muddy up the hop profile, but we also don't want it too scoured-out—balance can suffer in a beer this light if attenuation creeps up. Choose something that is clean or clean-ish, but without super-high attenuation. If you're a fan of Vermont-style IPAs, this is an ideal place for Wyeast 1318.

Hop stand, not dry hop: Allowing the hops to steep in the hot wort after the boil is shut down but before chilling extracts all those lovely oils and aromatics without the processing challenges that come with adding hops to the fermentor. We won't have to wait for dry hops to settle out or manage contact time on the cold side, and turnaround from brew day to packaging will be minimal.

BREWING

PREP
- Mill the grains. Then collect strike water and heat to 165°F.

MASH & SPARGE
- **Mash rest:** Add grains to strike water, mix to 151–153°F, and rest for 60-90 minutes. Collect and heat sparge water.
- **Mashout:** Heat to 170°F for 5 minutes.
- Sparge and collect the wort in the boil kettle.

BOIL *(60 minutes)*
- **T-10:** 0.5 oz. each of Idaho 7 and Mandarina Bavaria.
- **T-0:** 0.5 oz. each of Idaho 7 and Mandarina Bavaria plus 1 oz. Galaxy. Let steep.
- **T+20**: Cool the wort, transfer to a sanitized fermentor, aerate well, and pitch yeast.

FERMENTATION AND BEYOND
- **Primary fermentation:** 10-14 days total. Keep maximum temp in low to mid 60s°F. When activity begins to slow, allow 2–3 day diacetyl rest at approximately 70°F.
- Package once the beer is clear (use a fining like gelatin or Biofine as needed) and enjoy as soon as carbonated. This beer will drink best fresh!

TRE COOL IMPERIAL IPA

Targets: **OG:** 1.076–1.078, **IBU:** 80–82, **SRM:** 5.6, **ABV:** 8.2%

I knew a girl from San Francisco, and she and her Bay Area friends had been Green Day fans from their underground days. Then *Dookie* hit the charts, and no more. Mainstream success = kiss of death. A thing's coolness is inversely proportional to the number of people who like it.

Imperial IPA—in all its overstated, unapologetic splendor—is a nice parallel. With so many iterations, with paragons of the style flashing 100-point ratings online, inspiring rushes at the liquor store and lines at release parties. Hype, buzz, hoarding, trading, a grayish-black market—it's a lot of baggage if you *just want a beer.*

But, by the same token, popular things are often popular for a reason. "Who am I to blow against the wind?" Paul Simon asked, right before he went all corporate.

And as you read this, those citric, piney, stinky, dank hops in your LHBS are just waiting for a person of immoderate temperament to put an irresponsible amount of terpenes and myrcene and other volatile oils into a single batch of beer. Today, that person is us, citizens. There's plenty of room on the bandwagon.

American IPA is not a subtle style, and imperial IPA is American IPA's louder, good-timing cousin. But just because it's overpoweringly hoppy, doesn't mean it's easy to brew well. The hops need a solid malt foundation and a sound fermentation in order to sing and not merely clobber. Soapbox time!

In my opinion, the best examples of this style quietly exhibit some subtle malt harmonics—not quite multi-dimensional, but more than one-note. We need high-quality base malt with some spine to it— English pale malts, for instance, or a blend of domestic 2-row with English pale and/or a touch of Munich malt.

The best examples—again, my opinion!—are also dry and clean, signifying not just an appropriate choice of ale yeast strain, but a healthy fermentation, too. Too caramelly and sweet, whether through overuse of caramel malt or under attenuation, and your imperial IPA can turn cloying. There is a separate category for barleywine, after all.

SHOPPING LIST

- 12.5 lbs. English Maris Otter

- 5 mL hop extract
- 3 oz. Citra
- 2 oz. Columbus
- 5 oz. Simcoe
- 3 oz. Galaxy

- Wyeast 1056 American Ale
  (or WLP001, Safale US-05, or equivalent)

- 8 oz. plain white sugar

KEY POINTS FOR KEY PINTS

Good hops: Use the most primo pellets or whole hops you can get. For maximum flavor and aroma, it's appropriate to add them at pretty much every stage of the process. Though in keeping with the "hoppy, not bitter" school, heavy late-hopping yields the bulk of our IBUs along with a powerful concentration of volatile hop aromatics.

Mash low, use sugar: For a dry IIPA, a low mash rest and a little easy-fermenting sucrose helps ensure high attenuation. This ain't exactly a guzzling beer, but it shouldn't drink like a dessert wine, either.

Hop extract: This syrup-like resin dissolves completely in wort. Using it as the bittering addition, we lose less volume to vegetable matter in the boil kettle, maximizing yield. Neat!

Dry hopping: As anyone worth their pretzel necklace at a beer fest will scream-tell you, an imperial IPA without dry hops isn't an imperial IPA. Make sure your secondary fermentor can handle the volume, and prepare a mesh drawstring bag if you want to contain them.

BREWING

PREP
- Make a yeast starter. Mill the grains. Heat strike water to approximately 160°F.

MASH & SPARGE
- **Mash rest:** Add grains and 1 oz. Citra to strike water, mix to 148-151°F, rest for 60-90 minutes. Collect and heat sparge water.
- **Mashout:** Heat to 170°F for 5 minutes.
- Sparge and collect the wort in the boil kettle.

BOIL *(60 minutes)*
- **T-60:** 5 mL hop extract.
- **T-5:** 2.5 oz. each Galaxy and Simcoe, 2 oz. Citra, 0.75 oz. Columbus, and 8 oz. sugar.
- **T-0:** Cool the wort, transfer to a sanitized fermentor, aerate well, and pitch yeast.

FERMENTATION AND BEYOND
- **Primary fermentation:** Low-to-mid-60s°F.
- When fermentation is completely finished, rack to a secondary fermentor and allow temp to rise into the upper 60s°F. Add dry hops: 2.5 oz. Simcoe, 1.25 oz. Columbus, and 0.5 oz. Galaxy. Allow for 5-7 days of contact, or to your preference, then rack the beer off the dry hops, package, and enjoy immediately once carbonated.

EL ESTUPENDO SOUTHERN HEMISPHERE DOUBLE IPA

Targets: **OG:** 1.083, **IBU:** 68-70, **SRM:** 4.0, **ABV:** 9.0%

There's a classic *Simpsons* episode where Bart joins a scout troop, ostensibly as an excuse to use knives and set snares, but ends up bathing senior citizens who admonish him to "stay above the equator." Let it be our intention to forsake that advice with this recipe—we're not going above the equator.

Talagante, Chile is home to Patagonia Malt, where they kiln an extremely pale base malt from Andean barleys. In much the same way that the light color of a Belgian strong pale ale or tripel belies its alcoholic potency, the ultra-light color yielded by even this big a mash load of extra pale malt will be deceptive in the glass.

And then to the South Pacific for a melange of dank 'n' fruity New Zealand and Australian hops. A mixture of Rakau, Vic Secret, and Wai-iti combine for a myrcene-rich smog of peach and grapefruit, apricot and orange, passionfruit and pine aromatics. Heavy emphasis on whirlpool and dry-hop additions will make it juicy and fruit-forward while still imbuing it with a good amount of hop bitterness.

Illustration by David Witt

SHOPPING LIST

- 15 lbs. Patagonia Extra Pale Ale malt

- 2.5 oz. Australian Vic Secret   • 4 oz. New Zealand Wai-iti
- 3 oz. New Zealand Rakau

- White Labs WLP007, Wyeast 1335, or Safale S-04

KEY POINTS FOR KEY PINTS

Yeast selection: We want a strain that is hop-friendly and won't throw off a lot of competing aromatics; it also needs to attenuate well (sickly-sweet IPA is an affront to all that is good in the world) and clear quickly so the beer can be packaged and enjoyed while hop character is fresh and loud. 007, 1335, or S-04 all fit the bill, but feel free to go with your favorite.

Start fermentation cool: Aim to start it a degree or two cooler than the low end of the recommended range for your chosen yeast strain. This will accomplish a couple things: it will suppress ester production, which will help avoid sensory interference with all our wonderful hop oils in the finished beer; and it will slow the rate of CO_2 evolving from the ferment, which will prevent hop aromatics from being scrubbed right out of the beer.

SMaSH it: This only needs a couple minor tweaks to become a single malt-single hop beer. Consider making Vic Secret or Rakau the featured soloist, and adjust additions for IBUs accordingly.

Or stay above the equator: For a northern hemisphere DIPA, sub in a domestic pale ale malt like Rahr or Gambrinus, and use Mosaic and/or Citra and/or Ekuanot hops.

BREWING

PREP
- Make a starter culture 24-36 hours before brew day.
- Mill the grains. Collect strike water and heat to 163°F.

MASH & SPARGE
- **Mash rest:** Add grains to strike water, mix to 148-150°F, and rest for 60 minutes. Collect and heat sparge water.
- **Mashout:** Heat to 170°F for 5 minutes.
- Sparge and collect wort in boil kettle.

BOIL *(60 minutes)*
- **T-60:** 0.25 oz. Rakau.
- **T-15:** 1 oz. Vic Secret.
- **T-0:** Kill the heat and add 3 oz. Wai-iti, 2 oz. Rakau, 1 oz. Vic Secret, and let steep.
- **T+20:** Cool the wort, transfer to a sanitized fermentor, aerate well, and pitch yeast.

FERMENTATION AND BEYOND
- **Primary fermentation:** 64-66°F for 7-10 days. When fermentation activity begins to slow, warm to 70°F for an additional 2-3 days.
- **Secondary fermentation:** Dry hop with 1 oz. Wai-iti, 0.66 oz. Rakau, and 0.5 oz. Vic Secret for 3-7 days, then package.
- **Serving:** Snifter or Teku, with a good book and no place to be.

AMERICAN PALE ALE THREE WAYS

Targets: **OG:** 1.050, **IBU:** 40–45, **SRM:** 6.5, **ABV:** 5.2%

American pale ale is the style that, directly or indirectly, launched thousands of craft breweries as well as many thousands of craft beer love affairs. It's a liquid opportunity to reflect on where we've been, where we are, and where we might end up.

Here then, are three iterations for a choose-your-own-adventure brew session: a Classic Formulation with a venerable combo of pine and grapefruit from Chinook and Cascade hops; a New Wave version featuring the stanky citrus and mango candy of El Dorado and Azacca; and a Tropical punch bowl of lime, coconut, and peach using Cashmere hops and bolstered with some fruit extract at packaging.

All three start from the same grist of pale malt supported by a small fraction of honey malt and medium crystal, and fermented with a clean American ale strain.

SHOPPING LIST

- 8.5 lbs. Rahr Pale Ale
- 6 oz. Simpsons Medium Crystal
- 6 oz. Gambrinus Honey Malt

Hops & Flavorings (choose one)

Classic Formulation	New Wave Formulation	Tropical Formulation
• 0.75 oz. Chinook	• 2 oz. Azacca	• 0.5 oz. Magnum
• 2.5 oz. Cascade	• 1 oz. El Dorado	• 3 oz. Cashmere
		• 2-4 oz. peach, mango or coconut natural extract

- Wyeast 1056, White Labs WLP001, Safale US-05, or equivalent

KEY POINTS FOR KEY PINTS

Chico or bust: There are a few instances where a particular yeast strain is more or less synonymous with a beer style, and this is one of them. Clean, hop-accentuating, and with a good work ethic in the fermentor, the 1056 Chico strain is one of the most-used yeasts in craft and home brewing, particularly for pale ales and IPAs.

Specialty malts for color and balance: Domestic pale ale malt gives a nice, neutral base, while around 8 percent total of honey malt and a medium-colored crystal malt will give a deep gold color, flavors of sweet caramel and fruit, and counterbalance the rather stiff hop bitterness.

Lots of late boil hops, just a bit of dry hops: A good dose of late hops will give us pronounced but not screaming levels of flavor and aroma, backed up with just a modest bit of dry hopping—we don't want to take a hard left into IPA territory here!

Anglicize it: If you want to take this ale all the way back to the source, substitute Maris Otter or Golden Promise for the Rahr pale, replace the hops in the Classic Formulation with Challenger and East Kent Golding, and use a Whitbread- or London-type ale yeast to create an English pale ale.

BREWING

PREP
- Mill the grains, then collect strike water and heat it to 164°F.

MASH & SPARGE
- **Mash rest:** Add grains to strike water, mix to 152°F, and rest for 60 minutes.
- **Mashout:** Heat to 170°F for 5 minutes.
- Sparge and collect wort in boil kettle.

BOIL *(60 minutes)*

Classic Formulation	New Wave Formulation	Tropical Formulation
• **T-60:** 0.75 oz. Chinook.	• **T-60:** 0.5 oz. Azacca.	• **T-60:** 0.5 oz. Magnum.
• **T-15:** 1 oz. Cascade.	• **T-5:** 1 oz. Azacca and	• **T-5:** 2.5 oz. Cashmere.
• **T-0:** 1 oz. Cascade.	1 oz. El Dorado.	• **T-0:** Cool the wort
• **T-0:** Cool the wort	• **T-0:** Cool the wort	and transfer to a
and transfer to a	and transfer to a	sanitized fermentor.
sanitized fermentor.	sanitized fermentor.	

FERMENTATION AND BEYOND

- **Primary fermentation:** 66-68°F for 7-10 days.
- **Secondary fermentation:** 1-2 weeks.
- **Classic Formulation:** Dry hop with 0.5 oz. Cascade for 3-7 days.
- **New Wave Formulation:** Dry hop with 0.5 oz. Azacca for 3-7 days.
- **Tropical Formulation:** Dry hop with 0.5 oz. Cashmere for 3-7 days, and add 2-4 oz. (to taste) of chosen fruit extract at packaging.
- **Serving:** Shaker pint, front porch, feet up.

DOUBLE RED/SINGLE BLACK PARTI-GYLE

Double Red Targets: **OG:** 1.070, **IBU:** 52–54, **SRM:** 10.5, **ABV:** 7.0%
Single Black Targets: **OG**: 1.050, **IBU:** 42-44, **SRM:** 30, **ABV:** 5.0%

From one mash, two beers: a strong, hop-bursted, piney-slash-caramelly, dry-hopped West Coast-style red ale, and a putatively sessionable stout-slash-black IPA type of deal.

By splitting runoff from the mash evenly between two vessels, we'll collect two different worts of disparate sugar content and flavor intensity. The first runnings from the lauter tun will contain more of the malt sugars (approximately two-thirds of the total extract). So the first beer will be, in the parlance of our times, a hitter. It will have a higher potential alcohol and a stronger influence from the specialty grains—in this case, a nice array of crystal malts and malted oats.

The latter half of the runnings will contain the final third or so of the total grain sugars and a higher proportion of sparge water. Thus the second beer will be a slighter affair with a more tannic, husky quality, as well as a lower gravity, making for a quick-turning and thirst-quenching everyday ale. To add some extra interest to the small beer, as well as achieve a much darker color, we'll cap the mash during the last half of the sparge.

This is not a new technique by any means—brewing a series of successively smaller beers from the runnings of one mash has been employed by brewers for hundreds of years. Think of a monastic table beer made from the last gasps of a tripel mash, or a mild ale eked out of the tail end of a massive barleywine wort.

Now, it's our turn to double down.

Nota bene: We'll need two boilers for two concurrent worts, but the volumes will be pretty modest (about 3.25 gallons each) so we can get by without huge kettles. But given the shuffling of vessels and real-time management of two separate worts, it may be a good idea to round up a brewday co-pilot.

SHOPPING LIST

- 9.5 lbs. Rahr Pale Ale
- 8 oz. Simpsons Golden Naked Oats
- 1 lb. Patagonia Perla Negra (milled separately)
- 1 lb. Patagonia Caramel 15
- 8 oz. Simpsons Double Roasted Crystal

- 1 oz. Chinook
- 3 oz. Cascade
- 1 oz. CTZ or Columbus

- Packs of your two favorite American-style ale yeast strains
  (or, if using the same strain for both, one pack propagated in a yeast starter.)

KEY POINTS FOR KEY PINTS

Same yeast or different strains: For the sake of variety, two different strains for the two different worts would be interesting. Even though the Double Red is a high-gravity wort, it's also smaller volume, so we can skip a starter and direct-pitch a pack. Though if you have an all-time favorite strain (or don't want to buy multiple packs), just propagate one in a starter and split it.

Capping the mash: Adding fresh malt (usually a caramel/crystal or roasted malt) to the lauter tun before the sparge of the smaller beer boosts color, flavor, and body. The Perla Negra is added after the first runnings are collected, in order to darken the final runnings for the Single Black.

BREWING

PREP
- If propagating from a single pack of yeast, make a yeast starter.
- Mill the grains (keep the Perla Negra separate) and heat strike water to approximately 165°F.

MASH & SPARGE
- **Mash rest:** Add all grains except the Perla Negra to strike water, mix to 151–153°F, and rest for 60–90 minutes. Collect and heat sparge water.
- **Mashout:** Heat it to 170°F for 5 minutes.
- Begin sparging and collect ~3.25 gallons of the first runnings in one boil kettle—this is the Double Red.
- Add the Perla Negra to the top of the lauter tun and continue sparging. Collect ~3.25 gallons in a second boil kettle—this is the Single Black.

BOIL: DOUBLE RED *(60 minutes)*
- **T-15:** 0.5 oz. each Chinook and CTZ.
- **T-0:** 0.5 oz. each Chinook and CTZ.

BOIL: SINGLE BLACK *(60 minutes)*
- **T-60:** 0.75 oz. Cascade.
- **T-10:** 1.25 oz. Cascade.
- **T-0:** Cool both worts, transfer to separate, sanitized fermentors, aerate and pitch yeast.

FERMENTATION AND BEYOND
- **Primary fermentation:** Around 65°F. When activity begins to slow, allow it to warm up to approximately 70°F for a 2–3 day diacetyl rest (if needed.)
- Dry-hop the Double Red with 1 oz. Cascade, and allow contact for 3–7 days.
- Package both when gravity is stable, appearance is clear, and flavor is to your liking.

EXTRAORDINARY ORDINARY BITTER

Targets: **OG:** 1.036, **IBU:** 35, **SRM:** 5.8, **ABV:** 3.2–3.8%.

Citizens, if you're like me, you enjoy the process and ritual of drinking a good beer. We may even have in common that when the opportunity arises for a subsequent beer or beers, other obligations permitting, you will not shrink away from this serendipity. And if we share the same top-fermented spirit animal, you enjoy a good bitter.

"Session" has been increasingly used to describe various beers. The definition is a loose one, not to mention culturally dependent (real talk: session beer in Munich makes it hard to find your hotel). In my opinion, the apotheosis of session beer may well be English bitter—full of flavor, rich with tradition, and low enough in alcohol to facilitate sentence construction, answers to trivia question, accurate bocce rolls, and things like that.

Bitter straddles a whole range of color, hop level, and alcohol content (and the same beer might be a pale ale if bottled or a bitter if served on draft.) They are divided (with a certain amount of overlap) according to gravity and alcohol—the biggest are the extra special (or strong), followed by special (or best), and finally our recipe here, an ordinary (or standard) bitter, the session end of the bitter family.

With a name like bitter, hops are a defining component of these beers, but not to the levels American IPA aficionados might be used to. A low starting gravity means less hops are needed to convey a bitter and/or hoppy impression to the palate.

Although there's wiggle room in terms of IBUs, bitters are a balanced style—it's a hallmark of their drinkability. With such a small malt bill and low OG, the quality of the malt used is key to achieving that balance. It's hard to fake the funk with anything other than a good English pale ale malt for a base.

For a brewer, turning out a good iteration of an ordinary bitter is a bit like limbo—how low can you go? The scaled-down structure and ingredient list restrict volume in favor of tone. Let's go.

SHOPPING LIST

- 5.75 lbs. top-quality UK Pale Ale malt
  (floor-malted Maris Otter, Golden Promise, etc.)
- 4 oz. UK dark crystal malt (70–80°L or so)
- 2 oz. amber malt (substitute biscuit malt if amber is not available)

- 2 oz. dual-purpose English hops (Northdown, Boadicea, Challenger, First Gold, Progress, Sovereign...)

- Your favorite English ale strain—I'm going with Wyeast 1968 London ESB

KEY POINTS FOR KEY PINTS

Get the good malt: Using a top-shelf base malt like Warminster or Crisp Gleneagles will still be a small investment for a wort of this gravity, but have a big impact on the outcome.

Crystal & specialty malts in check: A very small percentage of crystal and "character" malts like amber or biscuit will lend color and depth of flavor without becoming overpowering.

Use a digital scale: For dosing out those small but important late additions, it's good to be accurate.

BREWING

PREP
- Maybe make a yeast starter. Mill the grains. Heat strike water to approximately 165°F.

MASH & SPARGE
- **Mash rest:** Add all grains to strike water, mix to 151–153°F, and rest for 60–90 minutes. Collect and heat sparge water.
- **Mashout:** Heat it to 170°F for 5 minutes.
- Sparge and collect the wort in the boil kettle.

  BOIL *(60 minutes, while practicing your Cockney rhyming slang.)*
- **T-60:** 1 oz. Northdown (or your choice hops.)
- **T-15:** 11 grams (0.375 oz.) more hops.
- **T-0:** 11 grams (0.375 oz.) more hops right after you turn off the burner. Then cool the wort, transfer to a sanitized fermentor, aerate well, and pitch yeast.

FERMENTATION AND BEYOND
- **Primary fermentation:** Aim for the mid-to-upper-60s°F—consult the lab's yeast profile guide for optimum temperature.
- When activity begins to slow, allow the fermentor to warm up to approximately 70°F for a 2–3 day diacetyl rest. (With a low-gravity wort, it's not out of the question to see fermentation completed within just a couple days, but don't be tempted to rack out of primary too early—give the cells a chance to clean up after themselves.)
- Secondary fermentation is optional for a "running ale" like this. Generally, it should be ready for bottle or keg around 10–20 days after brewing, but package as soon as clarity and flavor are to your liking, and drink it while the malt/yeast interplay is still juicy and the hops are snappy—i.e., as soon as it's carbonated. Re-brew as necessary.

NEW ENGLAND-ISH BITTER

Targets: **OG:** 1.044, **IBU:** 30–35 (nominal), **SRM:** 3.5, **ABV:** 4.7%

I hate to call this a session IPA, but you could if you had to.

It's a sub-five percent ABV, glucan-rich, non-"C" hop juice bomb. But it's really got the soul (or at any rate, the malt, yeast, and ABV percentage) of a lovely imperial pint–sloshing bitter.

Here's the plan: flavorful pale ale malt base (we're calling for Golden Promise, but Maris Otter would be great too) with a lauter-tun punishing load of malted oats. Nothing but whirlpool and fermentor additions of extremely fruit-forward hop varieties, ones that bring the melon, berry, and tropical flavors (versus something more strongly citrus/pine). Ferment with an estery yeast strain that makes a home in both UK and VT.

Illustration by Jeff Nelson

SHOPPING LIST

- 5.5 lbs. Simpsons Golden Promise
- 2.75 lbs. Crisp Malted Oats
- Rice hulls

- 3 oz. El Dorado
- 3 oz. Mosaic

- Wyeast 1318 London Ale III or Yeast Bay Vermont Ale

KEY POINTS FOR KEY PINTS

Rice/oat hulls are your friend: If you do brew-in-a-bag (BIAB) mashing, you can skip ahead—no stuck mash for you. For my fellow fly-sparging Luddites, add a couple handfuls of preventative mash filtration aid at dough-in.

Bitterness vs. flavor/aroma: This is designed for maximum hop flavor and aroma, with bitterness as a side effect. We'll get some amount of utilization/isomerization from the hop stand, but don't worry overmuch about calculating it.

Can't find malted oats? White wheat malt would be a good stand-in.

Other hops: Citra, Hüll Melon, Galaxy, or Vic Secret would mix in nicely at a 1:1 substitution rate.

Yeast: Strains of choice add complementary esters and texture to New England-style hop delivery systems: "Conan" and Wyeast 1318 are a couple options used by pros that are readily available to homebrewers.

BREWING

PREP
- Make a yeast starter prior to brew day. Mill the grains. Heat strike water to approximately 166°F.

MASH & SPARGE
- **Mash Resh:** Add all grains to strike water, mix to 153–154°F, and rest for 60–90 minutes. Collect and heat sparge water.
- **Mashout:** Heat to 170°F for 5 minutes.
- Sparge and collect the wort in the boil kettle.

BOIL *(60 minutes)*
- **T-0:** Turn off the heat and add 1.5 oz. El Dorado and 1.5 oz. Mosaic, and let steep.
- **T+20:** Cool it, transfer to a sanitized fermentor, aerate well, and pitch yeast.

FERMENTATION AND BEYOND
- Depending on the yeast strain being used, aim for a fermentation temperature in the mid-60s.
- When fermentation activity begins to slow, add the remaining 1.5 oz. El Dorado and 1.5 oz. Mosaic to the fermentor as a dry hop addition.
- After 3–7 days contact with the dry hops, rack or package the green beer—New England IPA brewers don't shy away from a little (or a lot) of turbidity in the presentation, so don't worry about finings or a secondary unless you're so inclined.
- This beer will drink best fresh, when the hop character is at its most pronounced—don't delay gratification.

HOMEGROWN WET HOP IPA

Targets: **OG:** 1.059, **IBU:** ~50, **SRM:** 5.0, **ABV:** 6.0%

Just by virtue of the fact that you're reading this, there's a good chance you have your own backyard hop garden, or know someone who does. Which further means that sometime in the general vicinity of Labor Day you'll have access to grocery bag after grocery bag of fresh, undried hop cones. Which, to carry this line of thinking to its logical conclusion, means wet hop beer.

This is going to look like a lot of hops for five gallons, and it is. But bear in mind that fresh hops have a lot of water weight that would otherwise be removed in the hop kiln. In terms of acid and oil contribution, one ounce of dried, processed hop flowers is equal to 5-6 ounces of fresh cones straight off the bine. Variety is up to you and what's available—obviously a hop like Cascade, Centennial, Chinook, or the like will be classic, but we can certainly turn out a very nice wet hop ale with Liberty, Willamette, or others.

But before we get to all that fresh, wet goodness, we'll use CO_2-extracted hop resin (aka hop extract) for the main boil addition. This will help us out in a couple ways: first, because it's, at best, very difficult to calculate IBU contribution from homegrown hops. Hop extract is a known quantity and will make the bittering addition much less of a shot in the dark. Second, we're already dumping in a lot of green plant material, and the hop extract will curb wort loss just a bit.

And before that, we'll establish a nice malt foundation with Maris Otter and a bit of English Caramalt for color and light toffee flavor to underscore the ripe, citric and/or herbal and/or spicy flavor of your fresh crop.

SHOPPING LIST

- 10 lbs. Simpsons Maris Otter

- 6 oz. Simpsons Caramalt

- 5 mL CO_2 hop extract

- 15-20 oz. fresh, undried hop cones

- White Labs WLP007, Wyeast 1335, or Safale S-04

KEY POINTS FOR KEY PINTS

Timing is everything: Have the other ingredients on hand and ready to go, and schedule your brew day to coincide with the cones' peak condition, when the yellow lupulin glands are prolific and sticky, and the bracts start to turn papery and lose a bit of their spring.

Harvest at last minute: Undried hops are extremely perishable and start to deteriorate as soon as they're picked; without drying to arrest the decomposition of the aromatic oils, they need to go into the beer ASAP. You could even wait until the boil starts to begin picking.

Dry hop if needed/desired: In the same way it's very tough to gauge bitterness contribution and alpha content of homegrown hops, the oil content can vary depending on variety, growing conditions, and other factors. Taste the beer after primary, and supplement as needed with dry hopping in secondary, with dried homegrown hops or store-bought of the same variety.

BREWING

PREP
- Make a starter culture 24-36 hours before brew day.
- Mill the grains, then collect and heat strike water to 165°F.

MASH & SPARGE
- **Mash rest:** Add grains to strike water, mix to 152°F, and rest for 60 minutes. Collect and heat sparge water.
- **Mashout:** Heat to 170°F for 5 minutes.
- Sparge and collect wort in boil kettle.

BOIL *(60 minutes)*
- **T-60:** 5 mL hop extract.
- **T-0:** 15-20 oz. fresh, undried hop cones.
- **T+20:** Cool the wort and transfer to a sanitized fermentor, aerate well and pitch yeast.

FERMENTATION AND BEYOND
- **Primary fermentation:** 64-66°F for 7-10 days. When fermentation activity begins to slow, warm to 70°F for an additional 2-3 days.
- **Secondary fermentation:** 1-2 weeks, and dry hop if needed/desired.
- Serve in a nonic pint grabbed with lupulin-stained fingers and drink amongst the late season hop bines.

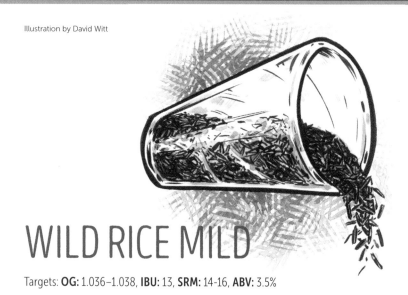

Illustration by David Witt

WILD RICE MILD

Targets: **OG:** 1.036–1.038, **IBU:** 13, **SRM:** 14-16, **ABV:** 3.5%

Here in Minnesota, there may not be a foodstuff as emblematic of our state as good old *Ziziania palustris*, better known as wild rice. When I think of our local harvest, I can't help but imagine how well those precious, nutty grains would impart a fine flavor to a dark mild.

Besides being indigenous to the Great Lakes and so culturally important to the native people of our region, it's highly nutritious—and not just for the drinker. Wild rice is rich in all kinds of stuff that our yeast cells will dig, like zinc, phosphorus, magnesium, and potassium. Its sweet, nutty flavor and body-enhancing proteins will be right at home in a dark mild.

Like many other adjuncts (looking at you, useless pumpkin), the wild rice won't have any enzymes to break down its starchy components into something fermentable. So we'll need to mash it with a good diastatic base malt. Cooking the wild rice ahead of time will accomplish some of the scut work for the malt enzymes and ensure a speedy, painless mash.

A dark mild will be our base beer. Starting gravities below 1.040 point to a final ABV around 3–4 percent, which won't crowd our showcase grain with intense competing flavors. The style usually pours in a color range of 12 SRM (pale russet) to 25 SRM (verging on black), so you might think of it as a little brown ale or a little porter. Bitterness can range from a very modest 12 IBU to a still-pretty-modest 25 IBU—we're going to keep it on the low end to ensure the malt and wild rice profile is this beer's centerpiece.

SHOPPING LIST

- 5 lbs. Rahr Pale Ale malt
- 4 oz. British pale chocolate malt
- 10 oz. Simpsons dark crystal malt

- 0.5 oz. Glacier (or equivalent)

- Your favorite English ale strain; I'm using Wyeast 1968 London ESB

- 1 lb. wild rice, cooked prior to brew day.

KEY POINTS FOR KEY PINTS

Any wild rice will do: This recipe was formulated with the standard, brown/black cultivated wild rice in mind. Substitute the hand-harvested, hand-parched version if your stocks
(and wallet) allow.

Diastatic power in the base malt: I'm calling for Rahr Pale Ale, a great all-rounder that will
easily do conversion work on the wild rice. If you prefer to use a more traditional English
base malt—like Maris Otter—make sure it has the diastatic power to handle about 15 percent unmalted adjunct.

Mash low (if you're me): "Malty" doesn't have to be sweet, so I'm calling for a pretty low
mash temperature to help our English ale strain attenuate well. If you'd prefer a beefier FG
and sweeter flavor out of your mild, consider tweaking the mash rest up a degree or three.

Don't oversparge: When brewing low-gravity ales, avoid the temptation to keep sparging
and sparging to hit the target pre-boil volume—that leads to tannin extraction and harshness. Instead, start with a more dilute mash and/or add top-up water directly to the boiler,
and stop collecting once the runnings from the lauter tun reach about 1.008 (~2° Brix.)

BREWING

PREP
- Cook the wild rice according to instructions prior to the brew session.
- Mill the grains, then collect and heat strike water to approximately 165°F.

MASH & SPARGE
- **Mash rest:** Add grains and the cooked wild rice to strike water, mix to 150–152°F, and
  rest for 60–90 minutes. Collect and heat sparge water.
- **Mashout:** Heat it to 170°F for 5 minutes.
- Sparge and collect the wort in the boil kettle.

BOIL *(60 minutes)*
- **T-60:** 0.5 oz. Glacier.
- **T-0:** Cool the wort, transfer to a sanitized fermentor, aerate well, and pitch yeast.

FERMENTATION AND BEYOND
- Aim for a fermentation temperature of 64–66°F. When activity begins to slow, allow
  the fermentor to warm up to 70°F for a 1-2 day diacetyl rest. By the end of the rest, the
  young beer should be clear and ready to package without a secondary.
- Our Wild Rice Mild will be ready to drink as soon as it's carbonated, and will be best
  fresh. Drink it before it's time to shovel snow.

BOCCE SWERVE HONEY CREAM ALE

Targets: **OG:** 1.049, **IBU:** 16, **SRM:** 3.2, **ABV:** 4.7%

My high school driver's ed teacher told my class that the mark of a good driver was a trip so uneventful it was not memorable to the passengers. Following that line of thought—a light blonde beer so smooth and perfect for summer, that your friends won't even realize they've been drinking it until their bocce rolls get all swervy and you crush them at ladder golf.

On paper, cream ale looks like a pale lager: straw-to-medium yellow color, mild bitterness, and a dry finish that will help offset a low hopping rate. But there's more going on under the hood of this indigenous American beer style. Cream ale was one of our few native beers to survive Prohibition, but no standards (in terms of yeast, ingredient bill, or process) arose from of the ashes.

It is categorized as a hybrid beer—fermented with either ale or lager yeast (or even both at once) and sharing some of the characteristics of each family. Its pale color, dry finish, and light flavors show some stylistic debt to American lagers, while some of its former sobriquets ("common ale," "sparkling ale," "present use ale") suggest connections to the English ale tradition. Almost all of them use some form of adjunct—whether an unmalted grain like maize or rice, or sugar additions—to help lighten the body and color, but beyond that, it's a bit Wild West.

Our cream ale here is no contemplative sipper—more of an unexamined guzzler. But it's always struck me how the most unexaminedly-guzzlable brews allow for the fewest goofs in brewing and fermentation. This recipe may disappoint those who count it a wasted morning when they don't have to pick hops from last night's IPA out of their teeth. But it'll tickle those who love a challenge.

SHOPPING LIST

- 7.75 lbs. Rahr Pale Ale
- 4 oz. CaraPils or Dextrin malt

- 0.75 oz. Cascade (or equivalent American hop)

- Wyeast 2112 California Lager

- 8 oz. clover honey

KEY POINTS FOR KEY PINTS

All-American ingredients: We love us some floor-malted Pils and Maris Otter, but keep them away from this beer—'Murica! I am using Rahr Pale Ale malt and Cascade hops, but substitute equivalents as you prefer.

Adjuncts for dryness: A lite lager-ish addition of corn or a British-y dash of kettle sugar would perhaps be more authentic, but I'm calling for some honey to help boost gravity and lighten body.

Clean profile from yeast: Ale or lager, the only mandate is that the finished beer be at most "lightly fruity" in terms of esters. A Kölsch yeast would fit that bill, but we're going to aim for super clean and neutral. I'm using 2112 Cali Lager for its clean flavor, temp-friendliness, and high flocculation—an American ale strain would work as well if you like.

BREWING

PREP
- Make a yeast starter prior to brew day—we want low esters and high attenuation.
- Mill the grains.
- Collect and heat strike water to approximately 160°F.

MASH & SPARGE
- **Mash rest:** Add grains to strike water, mix to 148°F, and rest for 60–90 minutes. Collect and heat sparge water.
- **Mashout:** Heat it to 170°F for 5 minutes.
- Sparge and collect the wort in the boil kettle.

BOIL *(60 minutes, while setting up your ladder golf set and preparing to issue a beatdown.)*
- **T-60:** 0.75 oz. Cascade.
- **T-0:** Kill the heat, stir in the honey, then proceed with cooling the wort, transfer to a sanitized fermentor, aerate well, and pitch yeast.

FERMENTATION AND BEYOND
- **Primary Fermentation:** Aim for a maximum temp in the low-to-mid 60s°F. When fermentation ends and SG reads somewhere around 1.010 (or preferably lower!), proceed with secondary or packaging.
- Secondary fermentation and/or cold-conditioning is optional, but will help stave off chill haze in the beer's youth.
- When the beer has cleared to your liking, package and carbonate to a healthy volume to enhance the clean dryness with some sparkly CO_2. Serve fresh and don't postpone joy, because summer is short.

WHEATY BROWN

Targets: **OG:** 1.055, **IBU:** 25–26, **SRM:** 20, **ABV:** 5.0-5.5%

Poor, unloved brown ale. It's not IPA, so almost by default nobody cares. It doesn't have the cultural cachet of Irish stout or Scottish ales. It's not mild or bitter, so the session beer trend seems to have overlooked it.

Let's embrace khaki. Let's make a strength out of standard gravity and malty brownness. Let's enjoy English-style yeast character, a full body, and caramel flavors. Let's also load it up with a truckload of wheat for a milkshake texture and a collar of foam that could float a quarter.

A southern-style English brown ale will be our general roadmap, but a good bit bigger. Southern English browns are sometimes described as a little bit stronger, bottled version of dark mild, or a weaker, paler sweet stout. They're sweet and caramelly from a combo of low hopping rates, high final gravity, and low carbonation. Crystal or caramel malts, plus some wheat are commonly incorporated. So we'll do all that, just more of it.

Especially more wheat—a higher-than-normal proportion in the grist will play up any bready, doughy aromas, and flavors that may be contributed by the yeast strain. Since wheat is so high in protein, its biggest impact will be on body and mouthfeel—think of the fluffy, billowy texture of a hefeweizen, and the impressive rocky head of cauliflower-like froth that tops it. That physical and visual sensation grafted onto the substantial flavors and color of a brown ale...well, doesn't trendiness sound overrated now?

Illustration by David Witt

SHOPPING LIST

- 6.5 lbs. Maris Otter
- 12 oz. flaked wheat
- 6 oz. UK extra dark crystal
- 1.25 lbs. Rahr White Wheat malt
- 12 oz. Simpsons Dark Crystal
- 4 oz. UK pale chocolate malt

- 0.75 oz. English Challenger, or the equivalent of your choice

- A malt-accenting English ale strain of your choice— I'm going with Wyeast 1469 West Yorkshire

KEY POINTS FOR KEY PINTS

Grain choice: Being a malt-driven beer, we'll rely on a deep blend of grains to stack flavors in this, the wheatiest and brownest of brown ales: Maris Otter pale malt and Minnesotan white wheat malt for a base; raw flaked wheat for body-building proteins and glucans; and imported crystal and chocolate for layered flavors of butter toffee, creme brulee, and light-roast coffee.

Yeast choice: An English-type ale strain with fairly low attenuation (for that high finishing gravity) and good flocculation (for easy clarification and quick turnaround) will be our friend. Aromatic contributions of fruit and/or fresh bread will be a bonus. Good options to substitute would be Wyeast 1968 London ESB or 1945 NeoBritannia.

Carbonation & dispense: If you have a beer engine or nitro system, this is the time to bust it out. A thoroughly degassed pint will enhance the velvety body and chewy maltiness of this beer to the point of making one cry. It will also take well to bottle conditioning given a low dose of priming sugar for a mellow, "real ale" level of carbonation.

BREWING

PREP
- Make a yeast starter prior to brew day (happy yeast makes browner ale.) Mill the grains, then collect and heat strike water to approximately 166°F.

MASH & SPARGE
- **Mash rest:** Add grains to strike water, mix to 152–154°F, and rest for 60–90 minutes. Collect and heat sparge water.
- **Mashout:** Heat to 170°F for 5 minutes.
- Sparge and collect the wort in the boil kettle.

BOIL *(60 minutes, while spinning The Band's second album.)*
- **T-50:** 0.75 oz. Challenger.
- **T-0:** Cool it, transfer to a sanitized fermentor, aerate well, and pitch yeast.

FERMENTATION AND BEYOND
- Depending on the strain, aim for a maximum fermentation temp in the mid-to-upper 60s°F. When activity begins to slow, let it warm to approximately 70°F for a 2–3 day diacetyl rest (about 10–14 days total.)
- Once the beer has clarified and is diacetyl-negative, it's ready for packaging. It will drink well as soon as carbonated, and will keep for a couple-three months in a cool, dark spot.

TWIN CITIES 60/- SCOTTISH ALE

Targets: **OG:** 1.032, **IBU:** 12, **SRM:** 14.4, **ABV:** 3.2%

Hogmanay (New Year's Eve) and Burns Night (or January 25), celebrating the birthday of Scottish poet Robert Burns, are prime occasions to enjoy the extracted essence of John Barleycorn.

There's no shortage of great Scottish or Scottish-inspired ales on the market. But I'm here to suggest a beer—a Scottish Light—that you may not have come across at your local taproom, and one that you can brew yourself and turn around in time to sip through a lampshade by the end of the month. A tartan plaid lampshade, mind you.

Because it doesn't have a lot of what helps the shelf life of a beer (e.g., alcohol and hops), it's hard to find authentic examples of this style outside their home country. This close cousin of English bitter—with a more malty, chewy character, and without the level of hops and yeast character—just isn't built for export.

Let's get this out of the way—it has the word "Light" in its name. It's a style low in alcohol, maxing out at a hair over 3 percent ABV, with many examples clocking in lower. I submit to you, citizens, that "light" and "low-alcohol" do not automatically mean "bland." If you can't shake the word association, call it a 60/- (shilling) ale—a reference to how much a barrel of this beer would have cost back in the day.

Even though there's not a lot to these ales, a brewer can still build complexity and texture through the selection of ingredients and a few tricks. It's important that what little we put in is high-quality and authentic—malt and hops from the UK and a good, malt-accenting yeast strain.

SHOPPING LIST

- 1 lb. English dark crystal malt
- 6 oz. flaked oats
- 4.5 lbs. English Maris Otter
- 3 oz. English roasted barley

- 0.75 oz. English Fuggle

- Wyeast 1332 Northwest Ale yeast

KEY POINTS FOR KEY PINTS

The right malt: Although traditional examples often use only a base of pale malt with a bit of roasted grain for color, a high-ish percentage of crystal malt plus flaked oats will add body and viscosity, keeping our Scottish Light from seeming thin, dry, and lifeless. Good alternatives for the Maris Otter would be Simpsons Golden Promise or Fawcett Optic.

Subtle hops: This is definitely not a hoppy beer, but a very light touch of late hops—just a quarter-ounce of Fuggle per 5 gallons—will add an earthy, herbal element to the deep, dark malt profile that the palate won't necessarily read as "hops."

Brown it: Brewers can (and should) caramelize the first runnings for a beer like this. Remove the first few quarts of high-gravity wort collected from the mash to a saucepan and boil them down by about half, then add back to the boil kettle. This intensifies the color and flavor, as well as the body and heft of the finished beer.

Alt yeast: I suggest Wyeast 1332 for user-friendly brewing and a clean, malt-forward, and full-bodied ale. But you could really ferment with anything from a full-on Scottish ale yeast, or an English or American ale strain. I even know folks who have brewed great Scottish ales with a Bavarian lager yeast.

BREWING

PREP
- Make a yeast starter prior to brew day.
- Mill the grains, then collect and heat strike water to approximately 170°F.

MASH & SPARGE
- **Mash rest:** Add grains to strike water, mix to 158-159°F, and rest for 60-90 minutes. Collect and heat sparge water.
- **Mashout:** Heat it to 170°F for 5 minutes.
- Sparge and collect the wort in the boil kettle. Caramelize some runnings, if desired.

BOIL *(60 minutes)*
- **T-60:** 0.5 oz. Fuggle.
- **T-5:** 0.25 oz. Fuggle.
- **T-0:** Cool it, transfer to sanitized fermentor, aerate well, and pitch yeast.

FERMENTATION AND BEYOND
- **Primary fermentation:** 60-62°F for approximately 7-10 days. For a beer of this gravity, transfer to a secondary fermentor can be optional.
- The beer will be ready to package after about 10-14 days, and will drink well as soon as it's carbonated. It's not built for keeping, so share it while fresh with friends and family for Hogmanay and Burns Night.

WEE HEAVY 140/- SCOTCH ALE

Targets: **OG:** 1.093, **IBU:** 30, **SRM:** 16-18, **ABV:** 9.0%

Hey, don't dump the dregs in the primary fermentor from the Scottish 60/- on the previous page—there's an awful lot of yeast in them thar buckets and carboys, and we're going to re-use it and do something awesome. Namely, jump a few steps up in the hierarchy of Scottish beers and craft a strong Scotch ale at home. (If you did already clean out your primary, no worries. Just get a new pack of yeast and propagate it in a starter prior to brew day.)

Scotch ale—which also does business as wee heavy—is the biggest, beefiest, brawniest member of the ale family from Alba. A note here on terminology: the high-gravity beers are always "Scotch" ale, like the whisky. The "Scottish" designator is used for the everyday-strength 60/-, 70/-, and 80/- shilling beers. Noted for their alcoholic potency and profound malty richness (think English barleywine or Bavarian doppelbock) this style is a vehicle for cereal grain goodness. These beers are meant for laying down in a cellar, sharing on special occasions, and considered sipping in a stemmed glass.

Our hefty OG and a typical FG around 1.020 or higher, combined with a low hop rate, makes for a sweet, powerful, and filling ale. Some folks like their Scotch ales more on the liqueur side of the sweetness spectrum, and that's stylistically valid, but I like mine a little more attenuated. The high gravity and low hop rate will naturally make for a sweet impression on the palate no matter what.

And also much like aforementioned doppelbock, a cool fermentation—an element owed to Scottish brewers' far northern climate—suppresses the fruity fermentation byproducts of other high-gravity ales, leaving the quality of the grain unadorned and lusciously pure.

Our Wee Heavy 140/- is more than twice the shillings as the Scottish Light, way higher in alcohol, and with a more massive shopping list. Bring a larger bag to your LHBS for this one, citizens.

SHOPPING LIST

- 16 lbs. English Maris Otter (good alternatives would be Simpsons Golden Promise or Fawcett Optic)
- 6 oz. English roasted barley

- 2.25 oz. East Kent Golding

- Wyeast 1332, or anything from a full-on Scottish ale yeast to an English or American ale strain will work fine.

KEY POINTS FOR KEY PINTS

Lots of yeast, don't skimp on O₂: Make a big healthy starter and thoroughly aerate/oxygenate the cooled wort. I love reusing the yeast from a prior, lower-gravity batch—it's like a yeast starter that you get to drink.

Caramelize the first runnings: Boil a few quarts of the most concentrated and sugar-rich runnings from the sparge in a saucepot, and add it back in before the boil. This will increase color and complexity in the finished product.

A little late hopping: The merest suggestion of hops late in the boil will add complexity and interest, without changing our drinking audience's read on the maltiness of our 140/-.

Stay cool, as the Fonz would tell us: Don't let this potent ale become headache juice—control the fermentation temperature. Slow and steady wins the race against undesired fruity esters, fusel oils, and higher alcohol. I like to over-chill the wort—aim for the upper 50s°F—and pitch the yeast just a tad too cold (the yeast will generate its own heat.)

BREWING

PREP
- Make a yeast starter, or ready the dregs from your 60/-.
- Mill the grains, then heat strike water to approximately 170°F. Given the size of this grain bill, you may need to adjust for your particular mash tun volume and make up the difference with sparge and/or top-up water.

MASH & SPARGE
- **Mash rest:** Add grains to strike water, mix to 150-152°F, and rest for 60-90 minutes. Collect and heat sparge water.
- **Mashout:** Heat it to 170°F for 5 minutes.
- Sparge and collect the wort in the kettle. Caramelize the first runnings (See: Key Points)

BOIL *(60 minutes)*
- **T-60:** 2 oz. East Kent Golding.
- **T-5:** 0.25 oz. East Kent Golding.
- **T-0:** Cool it, transfer to a sanitized fermentor, aerate well, and pitch yeast.

FERMENTATION AND BEYOND
- **Primary fermentation:** low-to-mid-60s°F maximum, for potentially 2-3 weeks.
- **Secondary fermentation:** 1-2 weeks before packaging (longer if you like.) This beer can be ready to package roughly 4-5 weeks from brew day, and will show best after at least a couple months of conditioning. It is built to last, so stash away a 140/- time capsule.

YOUR ZIP CODE GOES HERE ALL-PURPOSE BLONDE ALE

Targets: **OG:** 1.047, **IBU:** 18-20, **SRM:** 5.5, **ABV:** 4.6%

A craft beer snob's lite beer; a nonthreatening introduction to top-fermenting yeast for your macro lager-snob in-laws; a versatile companion to rest or activity; a simple but good beer that tastes best at its point of origination; an unfussy, fun beer. These are the diverse demands we're going to satisfy with this formulation.

Dank, piney notes from Simcoe hops will be recognizable to IPA drinkers, but not at a level objectionable to IPA haters. Domestic 2-row base malt is augmented with pale crystal and Golden Naked Oats for deep golden color and subtle notes of floral sweetness and hazelnut, and malted white wheat brings in some earthy, grainy flavor as well as texture and bolstered foam stands in the glass. Finally, an English ale strain for fast fermentation and faster clearing, so we can get around to enjoyment ASAP.

Illustration by David Witt

SHOPPING LIST

- 6.5 lbs. Rahr 2-Row
- 12 oz. Rahr Red Wheat Malt
- 12 oz. Simpsons Golden Naked Oats
- 8 oz. Weyermann Carahell

- 0.25 oz. Columbus
- 0.5 oz. Simcoe

- Wyeast 1968, White Labs WLP002, or equivalent

KEY POINTS FOR KEY PINTS

Like a pale ale, but not: Pungent hops, but in small doses. We're opting to use some varieties that are closely associated with more hop-forward and aggressive styles because they have desirable flavors—citric, piney, resinous—but we're just going to keep their intensity down to a more approachable threshold.

Low mash temp: A saccharification rest on the lower end of the range will make for a more fermentable wort, which will help offset the low attenuation of this yeast strain, and keep the finished beer light-bodied and sprightly.

Manage the yeast: Fermenting on the cool side will keep the esters of this ale strain at a pleasant murmur (think orange marmalade), and incorporating a temperature rise at the end will clean up diacetyl and hasten the completion of attenuation. After which, it will clump up, drop bright, and leave a brilliantly clear beer ready to package directly.

BREWING

PREP
- Mill the grains.
- Collect strike water and heat to approximately 161°F.

MASH & SPARGE
- **Mash rest:** Add grains to strike water, mix to 148-150°F, and rest for 60 minutes. Collect and heat sparge water.
- **Mashout:** Heat to 170°F for 5 minutes.
- Sparge and collect wort in boil kettle.

BOIL *(60 minutes)*
- **T-60:** 0.25 oz. Columbus.
- **T-5:** 0.5 oz. Simcoe.
- **T-0:** Cool the wort, transfer to a sanitized fermentor, aerate well, and pitch yeast.

FERMENTATION AND BEYOND
- **Primary fermentation:** 64-66°F for 7-10 days. When fermentation activity begins to slow, warm to 70°F for an additional 2-3 days, and package.
- **Serving:** Your favorite all-purpose beer glass, a frisbee, and bare feet.

BROCKENGESPENST ALT

Targets: **OG:** 1.050, **IBU:** 35–36, **SRM:** 16, **ABV:** 4.7%

> *They traveled in a motor-diligence out toward the Brocken.*
> *The brushland grew hilly and witchlike, clouds came from*
> *directions indeterminate and covered the sun. "An older sort of*
> *Germany," commented Günther, with a less-than-reassuring smile.*
> *"Deeper."*

Thomas Pynchon, "Against the Day"

Alt is a relic of a bygone era when Saxons hallucinated witches
and devils on mountaintops and everything was fermented by *S.
cerevisiae* and not *S. pastorianus.* Long after pale lagers conquered
pretty much the whole world, beers brewed the "old" way with ale
yeast still held out in pockets of northern Germany. But while Kölsch
became a bit of a darling for craft brew revivalists, altbier proved a bit
tougher for Americans to grok.

To brew an alt is to walk a tightrope between everything that's
wonderful about German malts and the *geschmack* of bitter hops, all
unobfuscated by yeast aromatics. It's also a balance between ale and
lager processes, with a specialized strain of *S. cerevisiae* put through
its paces at a cool temperature, and then lagered prior to packaging
and serving.

And since this recipe is all about the older, deeper sort of Germany,
we'll use an ancient grain to stand in for the wheat that can appear
in an altbier grist. Spelt (*Triticum spelta*) is a hard-kernel heirloom
wheat variety that has been cultivated in Europe since the Bronze
Age. It's quite high in protein compared to modern wheat varieties
(roughly 17 percent versus 12 to 14 percent), and, as you'd expect,
will do great things for the mouthfeel and foam of our beer.

The remainder of the grist will be a roster of usual suspects for alt-
biers. Let's get it on like Wotan.

SHOPPING LIST

- 4.5 lbs. Weyermann Munich
- 1 lb. Weyermann Spelt Malt
- 4 oz. Weyermann Carafa Type 1

- 3 lbs. Weyermann Pilsner
- 6 oz. Weyermann CaraAroma

- 1.75 oz. Czech Kazbek

- Wyeast 1007, or your choice of clean German ale strain (WLP029, K-97, etc.)

KEY POINTS FOR KEY PINTS

Yeast selection: You can use your preferred clean ale strain and have it turn out great. But for my money, Wy1007—a true alt strain from Düsseldorf—brings a wonderful bready character (think rising whole wheat dough) that makes it an unbelievable match with a Munich malt-rich grist. The one caveat for this—and most other north German alt or Kölsch strains—is that it's quite powdery. This means it will attenuate very well, which is great. But it also means the yeast will take its *Gottverdammt* time to settle out, which will require patience and perhaps finings and/or filtration.

What's with the Czech hops? Kazbek are certainly not traditional for a north German altbier, but with a lot of Saaz DNA they're not totally out of place either. Plus, Kazbek's remaining parentage from a wild Caucasus landrace hop really fits with our theme of old and weird—with maybe even a suggestion of the pagan.

BREWING

PREP
- Make a yeast starter prior to brew day—a large, vital population will help the ale yeast cope with the cool temperature at which we're going to ask it to work.
- Mill the grains.
- Collect and heat strike water to approximately 165°F.

MASH & SPARGE
- **Mash Rest:** Add grains to strike water, mix to 151–153°F, and rest for 60-90 minutes. Collect and heat sparge water.
- **Mashout:** Heat to 170°F for 5 minutes.
- Sparge and collect the wort in the boil kettle.

BOIL *(60 minutes, while hallucinating some witches and devils of your choosing.)*
- **T-60:** 1.25 oz. Kazbek.
- **T-15:** 0.5 oz. Kazbek.
- **T-0:** Cool the wort, transfer to a sanitized fermentor, aerate well, and pitch yeast.

FERMENTATION AND BEYOND
- Aim for a maximum fermentation temp in the low-to-mid-60s°F.
- Once fermentation has stopped and gravity is stable, rack to a secondary fermentor and crash cool to lagering temps. Lager for 3 to 4 weeks (or longer, if time allows) and use a fining like gelatin or Biofine as needed prior to packaging.
- Once clarified with a bit of lagering under its belt, our spelted Altbier will drink great as soon as carbonated, and keep reasonably well for a few months in a cool, dark spot.

Illustration by David Witt

STORM IN A TEACUP GOLDEN BARLEYWINE

Targets: **OG:** 1.140, **IBU:** 55-60, **SRM:** 9.0, **ABV:** 14.5%

Chevallier is to modern English malting barley what Black Sabbath is to contemporary metal—today's iterations all carry a bit of its fountainhead DNA. Apocrypha has it that it was selected (the barley, not Sabbath) in the 1820s by a Suffolk farmer from a land-race found growing in fields belonging to one Reverend Chevallier. Chevallier (the barley, not the reverend) became the first variety to be grown specifically for industrial-scale malting, and went on to dominate worldwide malt production for the duration of the 1800s. It fell out of use as its descendants, newer varieties that were easier to grow with better yields, overtook it; fortunately for us, it's been revived as a heritage barley.

Organoleptically, Chevallier is a different beast than modern English varieties we're familiar with (looking at you, Maris Otter and Golden Promise.) It's less mild, with a more pronounced bis-cuit-grainy flavor. It's more assertive in a dark grist, and adds depth in a pale grist—which will keep this high-gravity single-malt beer from eliding into one-dimensional boozy sweetness.

The single hop for this recipe is Boadicea, a dwarf hop with good bittering power. It's possessed of a great clovery fresh hay aroma that will be utterly lost in a beer this big and malty—unless, that is, one were to buy extra at the LHBS and reserve for dry hopping a bit before packaging day.

SHOPPING LIST

- 25 lbs. Crisp Chevallier Heritage Malt

- 3 oz. Boadicea
- **Optional:** 1-2 oz Boadicea for dry hopping (see Key Points, below)

- Your favorite high-ABV-capable English strain. Wyeast 1028 London, WLP007 Dry English, or Lallemand Nottingham would all be good choices

KEY POINTS FOR KEY PINTS

Make a yeast starter: That should go without saying for a beer this big. Or even better, brew a 1.035-1.040 OG bitter or mild with a single pack of yeast 7-10 days before, and reuse the second-generation cells from that fermentation for the big beer.

Second runnings = bumper crop bitter: By the time you collect enough wort for the boil, the specific gravity of the runnings will probably still be high enough to get a couple gallons of a bumper crop session ale. Cap the mash with 8-16 ounces of a pale or medium crystal malt (if so desired), then run in some more preheated mash water, and collect the second runnings to boil separately for a nice bitter or mild to enjoy while you wait for the main batch to mature.

That thing about dry hopping: We're going to want to let this one chill out for a while post-fermentation to let time smooth out the rough edges. If we want to incorporate some of that clovery, fresh hay Boadicea quality into the finished product, get an extra couple ounces when you buy the brew day ingredients, and dose into the secondary a week or so before packaging.

BREWING

PREP
- Make a yeast starter 24 hours in advance, or ready the dregs from a batch of mild.
- Mill the grains.
- On brew day, collect and heat strike water to 163°F.

MASH & SPARGE
- **Mash rest:** Add grains to strike water, mix to 149-150°F, and rest for 60 minutes. Collect and heat sparge water.
- **Mashout:** Heat to 170°F for 5 minutes.
- Sparge and collect wort in boil kettle.

BOIL *(75 minutes)*
- **T-75:** 3 oz. Boadicea.
- **T-0:** Cool the wort, transfer to a sanitized fermentor, aerate well, and pitch yeast.

FERMENTATION AND BEYOND
- **Primary fermentation:** 60-65°F until the specific gravity is stable, then rack to secondary.
- **Secondary fermentation:** 2-12 months, depending on your own patience and how the beer develops.
- **Optional dry hopping:** 5-7 days before packaging, add 1-2 oz. Boadicea.
- Serve in a snifter in front of a fireplace with good book.

Illustration by David Witt

BOURBON BARREL BALTIC PORTER

Targets: **OG:** 1.073, **IBU:** 35–37, **SRM:** 28, **ABV:** 7.5%

Beer historian Randy Mosher describes Baltic porter as arguably the true heir to English porter, because it's been continuously brewed for about the past 200 years. Taking its cue from 19th century porters, but of a stature more in keeping with Russian imperial stouts, contemporary examples can be found in the Baltic states, Scandinavia, and Russia; but also Poland, the Czech Republic, and the former East Germany. Bourbon, as if it needs an introduction, is American whiskey containing at least 51 percent corn and aged in charred new oak barrels. My favorites have a high rye percentage—which, by coincidence, would show nicely if paired with some dark malt character.

Let's bring those two great tastes together.

Baltic porters are littered with adjectives like rich, full-bodied, and complex. It's strong, but malty and sweet, with a fairly viscous final gravity. They have some overlap with doppelbock and schwarzbier—being a porter, there will of course be roast malt, but it's not roasty enough to be a stout. We'll need it to stop short of acrid bitterness, and the hop bitterness should be just enough to balance it all out.

In keeping with its provenance in Europe's cold north, Baltic porters are traditionally fermented with a lager yeast. If your basement, brew room, or fermentation fridge permits continuing that tradition, awesome. If not, a clean-fermenting ale strain will work fine.

SHOPPING LIST

- 12 lbs. Weyermann Munich
- 8 oz. Weyermann Carafa Type 1
- 8 oz. Weyermann Caramunich Type 3
- 4 oz. Weyermann CaraAroma

- 1 oz. Styrian Aurora
- 1 oz. Polish Lublin

- Wyeast 2124 Bohemian Lager, or your favorite all-purpose lager yeast

- 2 oz. Heavy toast American oak cubes
- Your favorite bourbon

KEY POINTS FOR KEY PINTS

Remember, roasty but not acrid: The dehusked Carafa I will make our Baltic porter dark but not stout-black, with licorice and molasses flavors but not French roast coffee.

American oak: It matches our bourbon infusion, though French or Hungarian oak cubes would work too. Heavy Toast is as close as we can reasonably get to charred oak from the shelves of your LHBS, bringing that caramelized and woodsy campfire quality.

Bourbon selection: High-rye and/or high-proof bourbons will have a bit more presence in the finished beer than a high corn or wheated whiskey. Follow your muse.

Eastern European hops: We're looking for some relatively exotic Slovenian and Polish hops for this recipe, but if you can't find Aurora and Lublin, then German Perle and Czech Saaz (respectively) would be good subs.

BREWING

PREP
- Make a yeast starter. At the same time, put the oak cubes in a clean glass jar, cover with bourbon, and cap the jar. Dispose of the remaining bourbon in a respectful manner.
- Mill the grains, then collect and heat strike water to approximately 165°F.

MASH & SPARGE
- **Mash rest:** Add all grains to strike water, mix to 151–153°F, and rest for 60–90 minutes. Collect and heat sparge water.
- **Mashout:** Heat it to 170°F for 5 minutes.
- Sparge and collect the wort in the boil kettle.

BOIL *(60 minutes, while reading some Gogol.)*
- **T-60:** 1 oz. Styrian Aurora.
- **T-15:** 1 oz. Polish Lublin.
- **T-0:** Cool it, transfer to a sanitized fermentor, aerate well, and pitch yeast.

FERMENTATION AND BEYOND
- **Primary fermentation:** Aim for a maximum temperature around 50–55°F. When activity begins to slow, allow the fermentor to warm up to approximately 60°F for a 2–3 day diacetyl rest. This should be complete in around 10–14 days.
- Drain the oak cubes (or not!) and place them into a sanitized secondary fermentor. Rack the beer on top and cool to lagering temps. Sample periodically during lagering to keep tabs on the level of oak flavor, and package the beer when it's to your liking.

MOTORBOAT OATMEAL EXTRA STOUT

Targets: **OG:** 1.065, **IBU:** 40, **SRM:** 34, **ABV:** 7.0%

One of my end-of-autumn rituals is fly fishing for steelhead with old friends. Solitude, no cell reception, deep woods, the loud sound of flowing water, wolves and eagles, aurora at night, nostrils full of the hoppy tang of balsam sap. After I return with a clear mind and a keg emptied of homebrew, my internal clock knows it's time to put away the rods and fly boxes and run the gas out of the lawnmower.

One year, waiting for my waders to dry, I was idly flipping through my recipe log and found an old chestnut originally brewed for a trip some number of fall runs ago. Much like favorite rivers and old friends, it's always good to renew acquaintances.

Like the name implies, you can't have an oatmeal stout if you don't have oats. This style, substantial but not night-ending, derives its full body and viscous mouthfeel from a healthy addition of oats to the grist. The oats are usually in an unmalted, gelatinized-flake form, but malted oats are sometimes used.

This being a stout, it has to be dark. Oatmeal stouts have their origins in England, so black patent malt is the roast grain of choice—it has a somewhat softer profile than unmalted roast barley, the roast grain of choice for the sharper, drier Irish stouts—which makes it a better match for the sweeter, more zaftig oatmeal stout style.

Because stouts feature such strong flavors from the roast grains, the role of yeast is often unfairly relegated to the backseat when planning a recipe. A good strain is able to tolerate the low pH of a roast-intensive wort, produce esters complementary to the roast-and-oat profile, and will attenuate just enough to leave a drinkable but still luscious and velvety-textured beer. Wyeast 1469 West Yorkshire Ale fits those requirements, and plus, it's what my tattered old recipe sheet says to use.

SHOPPING LIST

- 9 lbs. English Maris Otter
- 14 oz. black patent malt
- 1 lb. flaked oats
- 14 oz. Simpsons Dark Crystal malt

- 1.5 oz. Styrian Aurora (or equivalent)

- Wyeast 1469 West Yorkshire Ale

KEY POINTS FOR KEY PINTS

English malts—it's the right thing to do: Wilford Brimley wants you to use a good, powerhouse-flavor base malt and some nice English crystal malt, you guys. The nutty, toffee undertones will add three-dimensionality to the baking chocolate and grainy notes from the roast malt and oats.

Go early with the hops: I used Styrian Aurora in the original recipe—any other English or continental variety with a mid-range alpha acid content could comfortably sub in here. Whichever hop you use, limit it to the first part of the boil—we do want a good charge of bitterness since we're pushing the OG and FG, but oatmeal stouts are not known for hop aromas.

Let the yeast do the heavy lifting: Unlike a more neutral American-type ale yeast, we will get a lot of flavor and character out of the West Yorkshire strain, as well as speedy clarification and maturation. Like many English ale strains, though, it can produce some diacetyl during fermentation—remember to allow adequate time and warm enough temps at the end of primary for the cells to clean up after themselves

BREWING

PREP
- Make a yeast starter prior to brew day—this is a big beer and will need lots of yeast!
- Mill the grains, the collect and heat strike water to approximately 163°F.

MASH & SPARGE
- **Mash rest:** Add all grains to strike water, mix to 148°–150°F, and rest for 60–90 minutes. Collect and heat sparge water.
- **Mashout:** Heat it to 170°F for 5 minutes.
- Sparge and collect the wort in the boil kettle.

BOIL *(60 minutes, while wearing a nice pair of Merino wool socks.)*
- **T-60:** 1.5 oz Styrian Aurora.
- **T-0:** Cool the wort, transfer to a sanitized fermentor, aerate well, and pitch yeast.

FERMENTATION AND BEYOND
- If using the West Yorkshire yeast strain, aim for a fermentation temp of about 66°–68°F. When activity begins to slow, allow the fermentor to warm up to 72°F or so for a 2–3 day diacetyl rest.
- When the SG is stable and diacetyl has been reduced, proceed with secondary fermentation or packaging, as you prefer. This stout will drink well within a few weeks from brew day, and will last several months if stored in a cool, dark place.

STEAMPUNK ENTIRE PORTER

Target: **OG:** 1.055, **IBU:** 48-49, **SRM:** 30, **ABV:** 5.5%

Porter. Also known around my house as "Why don't I brew this all the time?"

Let's use our mash tuns and carboys to enter the realms of conjecture and apply some 21st century hop sensibilities and varieties to an Industrial Revolution-era ale, then ferment it as though we were 19th century West Coast lager brewers, for a Steampunk Entire Porter.

Forward! Backward! To the LHBS!

Our stylistic lighthouses for this batch will be robust porter and California common: the former a dark, roasty, chocolatey, bittersweet ale with Anglo-American heritage, and the latter an indigenous caramelly, hoppy, warm-fermented amber lager. Some of our targets will be the points (ABV, IBU) where these two divergent beers show some overlap.

But for fermentation, we'll take a cue from the brewers of Gold Rush-era San Francisco, who wanted to brew pale lager (as was the style at the time) but lacked refrigeration. Let that puppy run warm, and boom, California lager yeast came to be.

The net effect of Cali lager yeast plus porter wort—smoothing the rough edges of the roast grain, making it mocha-like and velvety, but still with a strong hop bitterness.

And honestly, we could leave it at that and have a very nice post-pumpkin ale, post-fresh hop harvest, post-Oktoberfest beer with which to usher out autumn—but naaah. More is more. Let's layer on a resinous, rosemary-and-mint overtone by way of some dank, new-school American hops added at the end of the boil. That'll make for one anachronistic, ahistorical Cascadian dark ale.

SHOPPING LIST

- 8.75 lbs. Rahr 2-Row
- 8 oz. pale chocolate malt
- 8 oz. Caramel 60L
- 8 oz. Black malt

- 1 oz. Chinook
- 0.75 oz. Mosaic
- 0.75 oz. EXP 5256

- A "California-style" lager yeast – I'll be using Wyeast 2112 California Lager

KEY POINTS FOR KEY PINTS

Help the yeast help you: Cali lager strains ain't exactly high attenuators. To keep our dank porter from seeming like a hoppy sweet stout, do the usual to help keep the FG down: mash at a lower temp, aerate or oxygenate the cooled wort prior to pitching, and culture a yeast starter to maximize yeast health and increase pitch rate.

Pair your hops: For the final hop stand addition, we're looking for a complementary blend of piney, herbal "dank" varieties with fruity varieties. Other good combos: Citra, Simcoe, and Amarillo; CTZ, Galaxy, and Vic Secret; or El Dorado, Centennial, and Chinook.

Ferment warm, but not too warm: The ceiling for most Cali lager strains is below 70°F, which should still be within the capacity of ale brewers without temp control at this time of year. These strains do not actually do well at true lager temps (roughly <55°F). Aim for a pitching temp in the low-60s°F and we should be golden.

BREWING

PREP
- Make a yeast starter. Mill the grains. Collect and heat strike water to approximately 165°F.

MASH & SPARGE
- **Mash rest:** Add all grains to strike water, mix to 151-153°F, and rest for 60–90 minutes. Collect and heat sparge water.
- **Mashout:** Heat it to 170°F for 5 minutes.
- Sparge and collect the wort in the boil kettle.

BOIL *(60 minutes, while polishing your cybernetic monocle.)*
- **T-60:** 1 oz. Chinook.
- **T-0:** Kill the burner, add 0.75 oz. each EXP 5256 and Mosaic (or the combo of your choosing), cover and steep.
- **T+20:** Cool the wort, transfer to a sanitized fermentor, aerate well, and pitch yeast.

FERMENTATION AND BEYOND
- **Primary fermentation:** About 7-10 days. Aim for a pitching temp in the low-60s°F and a maximum fermentation temp of about 68°F.
- Allow an additional week or so for clarification—this strain will drop quite bright all on its own (use a secondary fermentor if you feel it). Go ahead and package in keg or bottles once it's clear enough for your liking. It will be drinkable as soon as it's carbonated, with peak hop aroma at around 6-8 weeks, and will keep for several months.

OATMEAL CREAM DOUBLE STOUT

Targets: **OG:** 1.072, **IBU:** 35–40, **SRM:** 42, **ABV:** 7.5%

It's a bitter world out there, and that's especially apparent during the holidays. Cold weather, long nights, crass consumerism and cynical marketing, the parking lots and interiors of retail establishments, crammed like a vision of the end times in a Hieronymous Bosch painting.

All this puts me in the mood for something sweet, strong, and comforting, like Ryan Gosling in a glass. I'm talking about a high-gravity sweet stout.

Sweet stout (which sometimes does business as "cream stout" or "milk stout") and its close cousin oatmeal stout are members of a family of "nourishing" dark beers: full of B-vitamins and carbohydrates, relatively low in alcohol. We're going to obey the spirit of that law if not the letter, and go ahead and ensure our high-gravity fermentation produces a healthy level of Christmas cheer.

There are many paths to a sweet beer—controlling yeast attenuation, adding dextrins through mash temp or with crystal malt, and adding sugars like lactose with limited fermentability. We're going to use all of these today, and the result will not be subtle.

We're going to pack a little extra holiday weight onto the frame of a basic sweet oatmeal stout. First, extra helpings of base malt to overshoot the stylistic original gravity by a good bit. Then a double whammy of flaked oats and a good percentage of crystal malt in the grist—plus lactose in the boil—will collectively create a silken texture, full body, and chewy, viscous finish.

It's a stout, so we need a healthy amount of roasted grains for the black color and espresso/baking chocolate characte. A single hop addition at the start of the boil and a final alcohol content somewhere around 7–8 percent ABV, will bring some needed balance to the bittersweet equation.

This recipe would take very well to some aftermarket modifications—coffee beans, vanilla beans, oak, cherries, *Brett. brux*, cacao nibs—go nuts!

SHOPPING LIST

- 8.5 lbs. English Pale Ale malt (Maris Otter, Golden Promise, Halcyon, etc.)
- 1 lb. flaked oats
- 14 oz. roasted malt (see: Key Points)
- 14 oz. pale chocolate malt
- 10 oz. Crystal 120

- 1 oz. Nugget, Horizon, or similar

- Your favorite stout yeast—for me, there's no option for a full-bodied oatmeal or cream stout except 1318 London III

- 1 lb. lactose

KEY POINTS FOR KEY PINTS

The roast malt character—smooooove: Regular black patent malt or roast barley would work, but we want to lose the astringency to make some next-level Christmas Juice. (I'm excluding pale chocolate malt from this ban, because its 200–300°L is a good deal paler and its profile a good deal softer). Try Perla Negra Blackprinz or Debittered Black.

The bitterness—also smooooove: A roundhouse kick of hops would make our roast character seem harsh. Use a higher-alpha hop variety with a low cohumulone level. This recipe gives a range—go low if you have a sweet tooth, otherwise err on the high side.

The yeast—lots: With a good amount of unfermentable material to work around, our little guys need to be in peak fighting shape. Prep a yeast starter and stir plate 'em if you got 'em.

BREWING

PREP
- Make a yeast starter 24-48 hours prior to brew. Mill the grains, then collect and heat strike water to approximately 165°F.

MASH & SPARGE
- **Mash rest:** Add all grains to strike water, mix to 154-156°F, and rest for 60–90 minutes. Collect and heat sparge water.
- **Mashout:** Heat it to 170°F for 5 minutes.
- Sparge and collect the wort in the boil kettle.

BOIL *(60 minutes, to your best Barry White vinyl.)*
- **T-60:** Add between 0.75-1 oz. Nugget (see Key Points.)
- **T-0:** 1 lb. lactose, stir well to dissolve, cool the wort, transfer to a sanitized fermentor, aerate well, and pitch yeast.

FERMENTATION AND BEYOND
- Aim for a maximum fermentation temp in the mid-to-upper-60s°F. When activity begins to slow, allow the fermentor to warm up to approximately 70°F for a 2–3 day diacetyl rest. Depending on yeast health and fermentation temp, about 10–12 days total.
- Rack to a secondary fermentor, 1-3 weeks.
- This strong, sweet stout will be ready to drink as soon as carbonated, and will keep for many months in a cool, dark place.

RAS NECKBEARD TROPICAL STOUT

Targets: **OG:** 1.073–75, **IBU:** 38–40, **SRM:** 40, **ABV:** 7.7%

When we 21st century beer folks think of summertime seasonals, most envision something yellow and light-ish—Berliner weisse, Pils, or a wheat beer. But 19th century English brewers who sent their ales to the small latitudes didn't necessarily think the same way.

Besides the ubiquitous India pale ale, brewers shipped an awful lot of porter and stout to British colonies in the tropics. In the mid-19th century, porter accounted for almost twice as much of the East India beer trade as pale ale. Beer historian Ron Pattinson attributes this at least in part to class—the more expensive pale beer would have been for the officers, while porter was for the ordinary soldiers.

Even after independence from the UK, these beers remained part of the fabric of the local culture. In the footsteps of the strong black ales still brewed in Africa, India, and the Caribbean, let's make room in our buckets for Ras Neckbeard.

Tropical stout isn't a slight affair—with an ABV that can push 9 percent and commensurate body and mass in the glass, it can fall into the same weight class as stronger foreign stouts or even some imperial stouts. It diverges from both by a more laid-back use of hops (bittering only, no late hop flavor or aroma to speak of), rounder and softer roast quality (cocoa rather than coffee), and higher overall sweetness.

It's an interpretation of a foreign beer using a mixture of imported and local ingredients. Nigerian Guinness is brewed with a portion of sorghum, and Jamaica's Dragon Stout incorporates dark brown sugar, so we'll add a healthy dose of unrefined sugar as well.

Although strong enough to lay down, this tropical stout can be enjoyed as soon as it's carbonated, while its rum-laced charms and the warm weather last.

SHOPPING LIST

- 10 lbs. MCI Irish Stout Malt
- 12 oz. Simpsons DRC
- 1 lb. black patent malt

- 0.75 oz. Pacific Gem, Galena, or similar high-alpha variety

- Wyeast 2112 California Lager

- 1 lb. muscovado, panela, or piloncillo sugar

KEY POINTS FOR KEY PINTS

Sugar choice: Unrefined sugars retain more molasses from the raw cane and will give more character to the finished beer. Check the baking aisle, or your local Mexican supermercado.

Sweetness: We want some residual sugar in there, and we'll get it with a combo of low-attenuating yeast and high-ish mash rest temperature.

Complex roast character: The centerpiece of any stout. Roasty but not acrid, with some dark fruit and molasses notes. We'll get it from a good dose of black malt (instead of the usual unmalted roasted barley), double-roasted crystal malt (DRC), and sugar in the kettle.

Yeast choice: Not exactly British, but a steam-type lager yeast can be fermented warm and won't attenuate the heck out of the wort, for a boozy-yet-sappy and fat-bodied pint. It will drop bright quickly, letting us enjoy the beer while we still have some summer. If you want to go all-ale, 1332 Northwest or good old 1084 Irish would be excellent.

Substitutes: We want high-alpha and high-cohumulone from the hops—try Brewers Gold, Cluster, CTZ, or Chinook. Simpsons Double-Roasted Crystal is brilliant at reinforcing dark sugar flavors, but if it's unavailable, use an extra-dark English crystal (90–100°L).

BREWING

PREP
- Make a yeast starter prior to brew day.
- Mill the grains, then collect and heat strike water to approximately 167°F.

MASH & SPARGE
- **Mash rest:** Add all grains to strike water, mix to 153–155°F, and rest for 60–90 minutes. Collect and heat sparge water.
- **Mashout:** Heat to 170°F for 5 minutes.
- Sparge and collect the wort in the boil kettle.

BOIL *(60 minutes, while grooving to a Congos playlist.)*
- **T-60:** 0.75 oz Pacfic Gem (or your choice.)
- **T-0:** Add your choice sugar and stir to dissolve.
- Cool it, transfer to a sanitized fermentor, aerate well, and pitch yeast.

FERMENTATION AND BEYOND
- **Primary fermentation:** Shoot for mid-60s°F. Watch for activity to slow, and incorporate a diacetyl rest (increase temp to 70°F for a day or two) if needed. Should take 7–10 days.
- **Rack to secondary:** Condition for 2–4 weeks, then package and carbonate.

RYED IRISH STOUT

Targets: **OG:** 1.046, **IBU:** 33, **SRM:** 34, **ABV:** 4.8%

Dog-ear this page for February, so you can plan ahead for St. Patrick's Day with a New World twist on an Old World classic.

Dry stout, typified by Guinness and Murphy's, is a striking beer—jet-black with ruby highlights and a surprisingly pale head make for an appealing visual contrast. The aromas and flavors are a one-two punch of roasty and bitter, but with a soothing creamy texture. The disappearing liquid in the pint leaves lacy rings on the inside of the glass to remind you that you need another.

Our tweaked version will keep all that, but rye will add a new dimension—a little more earthiness (think pumpernickel bread) and a hint of wintergreen and herbal spice underneath. It's still going to have what many would consider another defining characteristic of dry Irish stout: multi-pint drinkability.

Unmalted flaked barley and unmalted roast barley are what make Irish stouts tick. The latter creates both the signature color and the acidic, bitter, coffee-like aroma and palate. The former, rich in gummy glucans and other high-molecular weight proteins unbroken by the malting process, is responsible for the aforementioned creamy-smooth texture. We'll replicate that texture, plus add earthy-minty notes, by replacing the flaked barley 1:1 with flaked rye.

It should also be noted that another tick-maker for our Dublin hallmark is the blending back of a small amount (3 percent or so) of pasteurized, soured beer into the final product for complexity and a bit of a signature "tang." We won't explore that technique with this recipe, but feel free to experiment.

Other possible riffs here might include:
- Replacing some or all the roast barley wih black and/or chocolate malt for a smoother roast profile.
- Replacing some of the roast barley with chocolate rye.
- Replacing the flaked rye with rye malt for a leaner, less silky body.
- Double the grain bill and triple the hop load to make an imperial rye stout

SHOPPING LIST

- 6.5 lbs. MCI Irish Stout Malt (or any nice UK pale malt.)
- 1.75 lbs. flaked rye
- 8 oz. rice or oat hulls (optional)
- 1 lb. roasted barley

- 1 oz. Northdown

- An English or American ale strain with a clean profile and good attenuation. I'm using Wyeast 1450 Denny's Favorite 50.

KEY POINTS FOR KEY PINTS

Rice or oat hulls! If you're brewing in an MLT with batch or fly sparging, consider including some. Flaked adjunct grains are gummy and cause stuck mashes, and a few ounces of prevention is worth a pound of swearing and remashing.

Just bitterness, please: Northdown is a wonderful hop, but we're only after alpha acids, so any workhorse, dual purpose, mid-range alpha hop variety from the UK or US is a viable option—Challenger, Northern Brewer, or the like.

No Irish ale yeast for an Irish stout? Since we want the rye to shine through, I am suggesting a cleaner-tasting yeast than my normal Irish ale strain. Wyeast 1450 won't produce the same amount of esters, plus it will attenuate well and help enhance the creaminess.

Nitro: Not necessary, but nice. A hypnotic cascade of bubbles resolving itself into a two-tone pint is understandably sexy for a lot of stout enthusiasts, myself included.

BREWING

PREP
- Mill the stout malt and roasted barley, or have it done for you at the shop. (the flaked rye and oat/rice hulls don't need to be milled.)
- Collect and heat strike water to approximately 165°F.

MASH & SPARGE
- **Mash rest:** Add all grains (plus hulls, if using) to strike water, mix to 151-153°F, and rest for 60-90 minutes. Collect and heat sparge water.
- **Mashout:** Heat to 170°F for 5 minutes.
- Sparge and collect the wort in the boil kettle.

BOIL *(60 minutes, while asking yourself why you don't brew stout all the time.)*
- **T-60:** Add 1 oz. Northdown.
- **T-0:** Cool the wort, transfer to a sanitized fermentor, aerate well, and add yeast.

FERMENTATION AND BEYOND
- **Primary fermentation:** About 7-10 days. Aim for a maximum temp in the mid 60s°F.
- Rest in primary for a couple-three-days after FG is reached, to clean up diacetyl and clarify, then package.
- Drink soon after it's carbonated—it won't see much benefit from extended aging. Just make sure to save some for your corned beef and cabbage.

Illustration by Jeff Nelson

BACKTHROW PRE-PRO TRIPLE GRAIN AMBER LAGER

Targets: **OG:** 1.052, **IBU:** 16–18, **SRM:** 12.8, **ABV:** 5.0%

By making use of some regionally grown grains (barley, corn, and rye—save that wheat for bread, yo!) we're going to brew a Minnesota-rooted beer that, when seen through the lens of a modern BJCP beer nerd, would be pigeonholed as an International Amber Lager:

"A well-attenuated malty amber lager with an interesting caramel or toast quality and restrained bitterness. Usually fairly well-attenuated, often with an adjunct quality. Smooth, easily-drinkable lager character," the guidelines prescribe.

In the grist, we'll use Rahr Pilsner, malted in Shakopee, Minnesota from barley grown on the Great Plains. We'll supplement with a big percentage of corn—the adjunct of choice when lager brewers from Europe immigrated in the mid-19th century, then some caramel and roasted malts from Bavaria for a reminder of the home those immigrants left behind.

Cluster hops are believed to be the oldest American variety, likely descended from a cross of some Colonial-era European transplant with a native landrace. They'll provide balancing bitterness and a suggestion of earthy, fruity flavor. We'll finish with fermentation via a Bohemian-type lager strain—but if equipment or temps dictate otherwise, go for a California-type lager yeast instead.

Let's throw it back, citizens.

SHOPPING LIST

- 7 lbs. Rahr Pilsner
- 8 oz. Weyermann CaraAmber
- 1.5 lbs. flaked maize
- 4 oz. Weyermann Chocolate Rye

- 0.75 oz. Cluster

- Wyeast 2000 Budvar, WLP802 Czech Budejovice, or Saflager W-34/70

KEY POINTS FOR KEY PINTS

Yeast health: In a beer where "cleanliness" of fermentation character is a virtue and there aren't a lot of strong malt and hop flavors to hide behind, we don't need any wack Sacch cells spitting mad VDKs and acetaldehyde. We will need a large pitch of healthy yeast and oxygen prior to inoculation to make it sing.

Long & low mash: The unmalted adjunct in the grist will benefit from a longer duration mash time. If you normally do a 60-minute mash, aim for 75–90 minutes for this batch. Additionally, a low mash temperature will help us achieve the high attenuation this style requires.

Dunkel-ify it! This could easily become an American dark lager by adding a bit of Carafa or even a few ounces of very dark candi syrup.

BREWING

PREP
- Make a yeast starter prior to brew day (alternately, use multiple packs of yeast).
- Mill the grains, then heat strike water to approximately 160°F.

MASH & SPARGE
- **Mash rest:** Add all grains to strike water, mix to 146–148°F, and rest 90 minutes. Collect and heat sparge water.
- **Mashout:** Heat it to 170°F for 5 minutes.
- Sparge and collect the wort in the boil kettle.

BOIL *(60 minutes, while quietly reflecting on Thomas Cole's "The Course of Empire.")*
- **T-60:** 0.5 oz. Cluster.
- **T-20:** 0.25 oz. Cluster.
- **T-0:** Cool it, transfer to a sanitized fermentor, aerate well, and pitch yeast.

FERMENTATION AND BEYOND
- **Primary fermentation:** Depending on the strain, aim for a maximum temperature in the low-to-mid-50s°F. When activity begins to slow, allow the fermentor to warm up to approximately 60°F for a 2–3 day diacetyl rest. Depending on yeast and temp, this step should be completed in about 10–14 days.
- Rack to a secondary fermentor and cool to lagering temps (a shed filled with ice cut from the lake would be authentic, but a fridge works too). Lager for 3–4 weeks (or longer, if time allows) and use a fine as needed prior to packaging.
- Package once good clarity is achieved and enjoy while fresh.

MÜNCHER HELL

Targets: **OG:** 1.049, **IBU:** 21, **SRM:** 3.3, **ABV:** 5.0%

The upside of a long-ass winter, citizens, is ambient lager temperatures in unfinished basements and attached garages. Let's harness Mother Nature's apparent hatred for us by using it to cold-ferment a Munich helles—a noble Bavarian lager we'll enjoy outside on the lawn when the grass finally does green up.

At first glance, it might look suspiciously like "yella beer." But let's take a cursory look at the brewing world of Munich in the 1890s: Its heritage was rich, dark, malty lagers—dunkel and bock—but Pilsner, the hoppy golden lager from the neighboring Czech state of Bohemia, was setting the world on fire.

Munich's brewers tried unsuccessfully to replicate that success with a pale, hoppy lager of their own. But the water in Munich is drastically different than the water in Bohemia, and while ideal for dark and malty, it was not suited to hoppy and bitter. So they settled for a pale, malty lager (helles, or hell, means "light" or "pale" in German), and it has been filling Krugs and Masses and Willibechers ever since.

Anyone who's been to a Munich beer hall knows that helles is meant to be crushed. Quaffability is a defining characteristic, so an emphasis on attenuation is key. *Malty* isn't the same as *sweet*, and with a low bittering-to-gravity ratio, helles can be at risk of turning flabby, cloying, and filling if a dry finish isn't planned for in the mash and fermentation. We're going for a grainy, slightly pastry dough-like aroma and flavor, and a low-level hint of hop flavor to support the malt and keep the bitterness to a murmur.

Helles is an elementally simple style: Pilsner malt, noble German hops, a Bavarian-style lager yeast. With an ingredient list that short, the quality of the raw materials is very important, and any defects or disruptions of the process tend to show through. It's a challenging style to brew, but that just makes swilling half liters in the presence of appreciative friends all the better. Come on, *wir brauen.*

SHOPPING LIST

- 8.5 lbs. Weyermann Pilsner malt
- 4 oz. Weyermann Carafoam

- 1 oz. Hallertau Mittelfruh (or equivalent)

- A Bavarian or Munich-style lager strain—I am going to use Wyeast 2308

KEY POINTS FOR KEY PINTS

Get the good malt: High-quality German Pils malt makes or breaks helles. You're worth it!

Get the good hops: Hallertau Mittelfruh, Hallertau Hersbrucker, or German Tettnang are all classic options for helles, while other good choices are German Tradition and Spalt. Just because this won't be a hoppy beer doesn't mean old or low-quality hops are good enough.

Mash low, aim high: I favor a multi-temp mash for beers like helles, in order to make the most of both beta and alpha amylase enzymes in the mash, to yield a wort that can be well-attenuated and dry without tasting thin. Though you can bust out a single-temp infusion (151–152°F or so) when time is not on your side or equipment won't permit.

Treat the yeast right: Disruptions or tics of the fermentation will show through. Big starter, plenty of O_2, and minding the fermentation temp will pay big dividends in the glass.

BREWING

PREP
- Make a yeast starter, mill the grains, and heat strike water to approximately 147°F.

MASH & SPARGE
- **Mash rest:** Add all grains to strike water, mix to 135–136°F, and rest for 40 minutes.
- Using either direct heat or infusions of hot water, raise the mash temp to 158–160°F. Rest the mash for another 20–30 minutes. Collect and heat sparge water.
- **Mashout:** Raise the mash temp to 170°F for 5 minutes, then sparge and collect the wort in the boil kettle.

BOIL *(60 minutes, while imagining the much warmer days when this beer will be ready.)*
- **T-60:** 0.75 oz. Hallertau Mittelfruh.
- **T-30:** 0.25 oz. Hallertau Mittelfruh.
- **T-0:** Cool it, transfer to a sanitized fermentor, aerate well, and pitch yeast.

FERMENTATION AND BEYOND
- **Primary fermentation:** Aim for a maximum temp in the low-to-mid-50s°F. When activity begins to slow, allow the fermentor to warm up to approximately 60°F for a 2–3 day diacetyl rest. Confirm that the beer is at FG (somewhere around 1.010.)
- Rack to a secondary fermentor and crash cool to lagering temps. Lager for 3–4 weeks and fine as needed prior to packaging.
- Our helles will be ready for *zum Wohl* roughly 6–8 weeks from brewing day; stored cool and away from light, it should stay in good condition for several months. Maybe even long enough for us to get what passes for a suntan.

OLDTOBERFEST SMOKED RYE LAGER

Targets: **OG:** 1.053, **IBU:** 28–30, **SRM:** 12.5, **ABV:** 5.1%

I remember drinking an Oktoberfest by Summit Brewing in July of 2014 and feeling like it stole my thunder. I was totally going to brew one myself, but now, why bother? What to do in the face of such reckless seasonal creep? Drink more Oktoberfest from cans and color outside the lines in the carboy, I guess.

Oktoberfest as we know it is an all-barley beer, and a showcase for that famous Bavarian malt character, clean and bright, filtered to brilliant clarity. But back in the day, this would not have been the case. The ancestral landbier of the village brewery would have been a chewy-textured, brownish-red affair, rich with grain and yeast, and almost certainly brewed with malts from a variety of cereals, which would have been dried over a smoky fire.

Let's take apart an amber lager and put it back together in a way that's historically inspired, even if not perfectly historically accurate.

For our throwback lager, a hefty percentage of malted rye in the grist will build a complex bready, earthy, slightly spicy flavor, and create a terrific density and texture. A small percentage of smoked malt will add a hint of woodsy warmth (but it's going to be subtle, so feel free to sub it out for more Munich malt.)

I'm calling for Weyermann Rauchmalz, which is smoked over beechwood logs at their plant in Bamberg as it has been for hundreds of years. It'll add a whiff of authenticity to our recipe, although at a much, much lower intensity than at a brewpub in Bamberg. The remaining color malts—crystal, dark crystal, and roasted rye—add the remainder of the color and bring in notes of toffee, breadcrust, and light coffee.

Just to keep it mixed up, we'll make use of newer, higher-alpha German hop varieties (brewer's choice!) to hit our IBU target with less vegetal material in the kettle, and a new world lager yeast (cold ferment not required—after all, ye olde village brewery didn't have glycol-cooled tanks).

SHOPPING LIST

- 5 lbs. Weyermann Rye Malt
- 10 oz. Weyermann Rauchmalt (beechwood smoked)
- 2 oz. Weyermann CaraAroma
- 4.5 lbs. German Munich malt
- 6 oz. Weyermann Caramunich Type 2
- 1 oz. Weyermann Chocolate Rye
- A couple handfuls of rice or oat hulls (optional—see Key Points)

- 1 oz. German Opal, Perle, or Tradition (or equivalent)

- Wyeast 2112 California Lager

KEY POINTS FOR KEY PINTS:

Beechwood smoked, not beechwood aged: This recipe was designed around Weyermann's beechwood-smoked Rauchmalz. You may find malt smoked over other woods or substances in the grain room of you LHBS (cherrywood, peat, etc.—Weyermann also makes an oak-smoked wheat malt) so pay attention to the label. I always encourage exploration and tweaking, but know that the smoke intensity and character will be different than planned (which may not be a bad thing!)

Don't like smoked beers? Feel free to replace the Rauchmalz with more Munich malt, 1:1. Everything else stays the same.

A few ounces of rice/oat hulls = a few pounds of cure: Rye is rich in glucans, a family of very gummy proteins that does amazing things for beer body and head retention, which can also play hell with runoff from your mash tun. Rice or oat hulls are cheap insurance!

BREWING

PREP
- Make a yeast starter prior to brew day.
- Mill the grains and heat strike water to approximately 163°F.

MASH & SPARGE
- **Mash rest:** Add all grains (and oat/rice hulls, if using) to strike water, mix to 149–151°F, and rest for 60–90 minutes. Collect and heat sparge water.
- **Mashout:** Heat it to 170°F for 5 minutes.
- Sparge and collect the wort in the boil kettle.

BOIL *(60 minutes, while dusting off your biggest ceramic krug.)*
- **T-60:** 1 oz. Opal (or your choice.)
- **T-0:** Cool it, transfer to a sanitized fermentor, aerate well, and pitch yeast.

FERMENTATION AND BEYOND
- Aim for a fermentation temp of 60–62°F, if possible (a bit warmer or cooler than this won't hurt). Depending on yeast and temp, this step should be completed in about 7–10 days.
- Rack to a secondary fermentor and allow to settle for 1–2 weeks before packaging.
- Oldtoberfest may not beat any commercial O-fests into your fridge this year, but it will be ready to enjoy as soon as it's carbonated and drink well through the rest of the fall.

MÄRZENBIER

Targets: **OG:** 1.057, **IBU:** 26, **SRM:** 7–14, **ABV:** 5.6%

If you'll indulge me a bit of autobiography, Oktoberfest (the lager style, not the party) was one of the reasons I started brewing.

Its clarity in the glass and its purity of flavor seemed so alchemical to a brewer of five-gallon batches of ale. The tubby red-cheeked Maß-guzzlers on the label (Paulaner, circa mid-1990s) put forth the intriguing notion of consumption by the liter. The timing of its release coincided with one of my favorite seasons. The rich but dry maltiness of Oktoberfest was too compelling to ignore.

Why am I calling this O-fest a Märzenbier? You'll have to indulge me again—we have to go back in time to when the cities of Vienna and Munich intersected with extra-long lagering periods.

In our **Oldtoberfest Smoked Rye Lager** (pg. 88) we explored the ancestral village version of a landbier. But the more familiar festbier of today is based on the more modern Vienna lager: golden-amber, a bit lower ABV but higher hop character than our O-fest, and making use of Vienna malt (a toasty, delicious midway point between Pils malt and Munich malt.)

Thanks to an exchange of brewing knowledge and technology between Vienna's Anton Dreher and Munich's Gabriel Sedlmayr in the 1840s, Bavarian brewers came to adopt a bigger vollbier-strength version of Dreher's Vienna lager as the seasonal festbier of choice for autumn harvest festivals. At some point further on, it became recognized as a style in its own right, taking its name from the annual festival at which it filled mugs.

For the drinker, Märzen is functionally just a shorter name for Oktoberfest. But for the brewer, its seasonality and length of lagering make it a distinct subspecies.

Märzen recalls a time when it wasn't possible to brew lagers outside of wintertime—too many microbes in the spring and summer air, with a temp in the cellars too ester-friendly. The last brews of the year were conducted in March, and left in ice-filled caves to lager through the summer, and tapped for harvest celebrations.

How bucolic! Let's brew!

SHOPPING LIST

- 10 lbs. German Vienna malt
- 6 oz. Weyermann CaraRed

- 1.5 oz. German Tradition

- Wyeast 2633 Oktoberfest Lager (or a warm-tolerant alternative— see Key Points, below)

KEY POINTS FOR KEY PINTS

Broken record, German malt: Good malt is vital for a malt-driven style like this. Spring for a top-shelf German Vienna malt, and your Krugs and Willibechers will thank you this fall.

Broken record, happy yeast Earlier I used "alchemical" to describe a wort transformed by lager yeast. A good lager strain shouldn't vanish without a trace, but it should leave a little mystery. We'll need a big colony of cells in peak condition—make a starter, give the wort 8–12 ppm dissolved O_2 prior to pitching, and mind the fermentation temp!

Long, cold lagering phase: The most defining feature of a Märzen is several months in a carboy or corny keg at 35–40°F. That'll make a bright, haze-free, clean and snappy lager worth waiting for.

If you can't ferment or lager at cold temperature: Go with a more temp-tolerant lager strain, like 2124 Bohemian Lager or 2112 California Lager, and don't plan to wait 'til September to enjoy.

BREWING

PREP
- Make a yeast starter, mill the grains, and heat strike water to approximately 165°F.

MASH & SPARGE
- **Mash rest:** Add all grains to strike water, mix to 151–153°F, and rest for 60–90 minutes. Collect and heat sparge water.
- **Mashout:** heat it to 170°F for 5 minutes.
- Sparge and collect the wort in the boil kettle.
- Add 1.5 oz Tradition hops to the boil kettle as the wort collects.

BOIL *(60 minutes, while regretfully packing away your 3-liter glass boots until September.)*
- **T-0:** Cool it, transfer to a sanitized fermentor, aerate or oxygenate, and pitch yeast.

FERMENTATION AND BEYOND
- **Primary fermentation:** Aim for pitching at 50°F and fermenting at 52–54°F. The beer should be at or within a few points of terminal gravity within about 14 days. Given the length of the lagering phase, don't worry about a diacetyl rest.
- **Rack to secondary:** Lower down to roughly 34–38°F for lagering—then do your best to forget it's there.
- Our Märzen could be packaged after about 7–8 weeks of lagering if you need to free up carboy space, but should still be stored cold until your own personal Oktoberfest is ready to kick off.

LAGERS

MINNESOTA COMMON

Targets: **OG:** 1.052, **IBU:** 45, **SRM:** 8, **ABV:** 4.8%

"I wish that there were just two more months in the year when we could stand outside like this," my wife remarked. We were straddling bikes in front of the school after dropping off our daughter. We were not wearing pac boots.

"Two more months of school?" I asked, misreading the situational clues, as usual.

"No, two more months of not freezing our asses off," she replied

Late spring induces seasonal amnesia and fogs the memory of night-plow routes. It's the point in the season when everybody comes out blinking into the lengthening day to lay eyes upon neighbors and sidewalks and lawns we haven't seen in a while. To celebrate the arrival of summer, let's brew a local-ish steam lager to enjoy while cleaning out the cabin, putting in the dock, and exposing pallid flesh to the sun.

Steam beer, or California common as it's technically called, is a hybrid style: a lager fermented warm with a specialized strain of yeast. It's a mid-weight beer, perfect for this time of year, where we're not that far past the last frost and nights can still get a little cool. This style calls for pronounced hop bitterness, which, in our iteration, will ideally come from locally grown hops.

The "steam" sobriquet applied to this style originally referred to the lively condition the beer had when tapped—a result of brewers in Gold Rush-era California creating hoppy lagers without refrigeration. Over time, the lager strains they used adapted to warmer temperatures and shallow fermentors (Anchor Steam, the modern-day archetype of California common, is still made in open coolship-type fermenting vessels.) The strains became their own subset of the lager yeast family, able to maintain a clean, crisp lager character at fermentation temperatures into the upper 60-degree range and nicely flocculate to create a clear beer quickly. This is the type of yeast we'll want to get for our Minnesota Common.

Simultaneously caramelly and hop-bitter, clean like a lager but fermented warm like an ale—this will be fun.

SHOPPING LIST

- 8.75 lbs. Rahr Pale Ale
- 0.75 lbs. Briess Caramel 60

- 1 oz. Hop Head Farms Magnum (or sub your local hops, see below)

- Wyeast 2112 California Lager

KEY POINTS FOR KEY PINTS

Local hops: I'm calling for Magnum from Hop Head Farms in Michigan (available pelletized at some LHBS) for the sake of formulating with a known alpha acid content. However, if you have homegrown hops, fire at will! Unless you have a good feel for their bittering potential, it may be advisable to reserve them for late additions and use a store-bought option for the bittering addition.

BREWING

PREP
- Make a yeast starter prior to brew day to ensure quick fermentation, good flocculation, and clean flavor.
- Mill the grains, then heat strike water to approximately 165°F.

MASH & SPARGE
- **Mash rest:** Add all grains to strike water, mix to 151–153°F, and rest 60–90 minutes. Collect and heat sparge water.
- **Mashout:** heat it to 170°F for 5 minutes.
- Sparge and collect the wort in the boil kettle.

BOIL *(60 minutes, while applying sunblock to your feet prior to donning Tevas.)*
- **T-60:** 0.5 oz. Magnum.
- **T-20:** 0.25 oz. Magnum.
- **T-10:** 0.25 oz. Magnum.
- **T-0:** Cool it, transfer to a sanitized fermentor, aerate well, and pitch yeast.

FERMENTATION AND BEYOND
- **Primary fermentation:** Aim for a temperature around 60–64°F. When activity ceases and gravity is stable, allow a couple extra days for the yeast to settle, and then proceed with packaging.
- Our Minnesota Common will drink well while fresh and should be thoroughly savored for the brief time it lasts, just like summer.

HELLADOPPEL PALE BOCK

Targets: **OG:** 1.092, **IBU:** 26–27, **SRM:** 7.6, **ABV:** 9.0%+

Pale doppelbock. We're going to do this.

Because I love comparative beer analogies, picture the pale bock as a traditional dark doppelbock without the raisiny, fruity, toffee, cafe au lait character, or as an even bigger version of a Maibock. It might even be compared to a lightly hopped Belgian strong ale, but instead of all the yeasty phenols and spice there are just waves of luscious, unobfuscated, slow-fermented Pils malt washing over your sinuses.

Like many other Bavarian beer styles, it's all about that malt, 'bout that malt—no hops. In a traditional dark doppelbock, the malt (of which it is all about) would be the more highly kilned and bready Munich. For a lighter-colored helles or Maibock—as well as this Helladoppel—the malt needs to be paler. Let's recruit a fine German Pils malt to do the heavy lifting.

Hops aren't entirely absent, though. Bavaria is home to a number of landrace, noble, and new hop varieties that native brewers use to balance their malty beers. In terms of flavor and aroma, hops in a doppelbock take a backseat (maybe even more like skitching on the bumper), but bitterness remains an important supporting element. I'm calling for German Perle, but any continental variety with mid-range alpha acid content—Tradition, Opal, Premiant, etc.—could happily stand in.

The key differentiator between doppelbocks and other big beers is the fermentation—it's a lager, so cool and slow is the name of the game. We want little to no fermentation esters and a smooth alcohol character. We want something "clean."

The challenge to the brewer is keeping yeast cells happy in a less-than-happy environment, e.g., low temperature, a high concentration of ethanol, increased difficulty in getting oxygen into solution, decreased bioavailability of nutrients, and high osmotic pressure as a result of the immense OG. Stressed yeast working through high gravity wort results in high ester production and harsh fusel alcohols—aka, not "clean." I'll say it now and forever: prepare a yeast starter.

SHOPPING LIST

- 15.5 lbs. Weyermann Pilsner
- 8 oz. Weyermann Caramunich Type 1

- 1.25 oz. German Perle

- Your favorite high-gravity capable lager strain—try Wyeast 2124 Bohemian Lager or Saflager W-34/70

KEY POINTS FOR KEY PINTS

Yeast health: A doppelbock wort is like a heavyweight title fight for yeast. Make a starter, maybe with some yeast nutrient, and thoroughly aerate or oxygenate the cooled wort.

Attenuation: Each half liter of this beer will contain close to a half pound of cereal grain. But the sweetness should come from a lascivious use of barley, not from under-attenuated wort. In addition to the starter, oxygen, and nutrient, mash at a low temperature for a highly fermentable wort full of simple sugars and a lower final gravity.

Slow, cool ferment: Controlling the rate of cell growth and fermentation is a big lever to minimize the production of esters and other metabolic byproducts we don't like in doppelbock.

Warm ferment alternatives: If your basement or refrigeration situation won't allow steady primary fermentation temps of 50–55°F, consider a California common-type lager strain, which will produce a nice clean beer at up to about 68°F.

BREWING

PREP
- Make a yeast starter, mill the grains, heat strike water to approximately 160°F.

MASH & SPARGE
- **Mash rest:** Add all grains to strike water, mix to 146–148°F, and rest 60–90 minutes. Collect and heat sparge water.
- **Mashout:** Heat it to 170°F for 5 minutes.
- Sparge and collect the wort in the boil kettle.

BOIL *(60 minutes, while stealthily adjusting your lederhosen.)*
- **T-60:** 1.25 oz. Perle.
- **T-0:** Cool it, transfer to a sanitized fermentor, aerate well, and pitch yeast.

FERMENTATION AND BEYOND
- **Primary fermentation:** Depending on the strain, aim for a maximum temperature in the low-to-mid-50s°F. When activity begins to slow, allow the fermentor to warm up to approximately 58°F for a 2–3 day diacetyl rest and ensure attenuation is complete. This step should be completed in about 10–14 days.
- Rack to a secondary fermentor and further cool to lagering temp of 32–38°F. Lager for at least eight weeks, although as much as a few months wouldn't hurt it none.
- Package when it tells you it's ready and imbibe with justified and unabashed enjoyment. Stored cold, this strong lager will keep well until next winter, at least.

LAGERS

SUDKRUEZ PILS

Targets: **OG:** 1.047, **IBU:** 35-40, **SRM:** 2–5, **ABV:** 4.9%

If it's winter in Minnesota—and as you read this, citizens, there's a better than average chance it is—then for many of us home-brewers it is lager season.

Lager is characterized in the brewery by slow, cold fermentation by a specialized subset of *Saccharomyces*. The exact taxonomy has shifted over time—it's known variously as *S. carlsbergensis, S. uvarum*, and most recently *S. pastorianus*. These strains have a higher tolerance for cold temperatures than their ale-making cousins over in *S. cerevisiae*. Their ability to completely ferment the sugars raffinose and melibiose **pushes glasses up bridge of nose** and a tendency to produce low levels of esters and phenols, creates the characteristic "clean" profile of beers like helles, Märzen, bock, and this Pilsner.

Pilsner is the most international of beers. Originating from and named for the town of Plzen, in the Czech Republic, Pils (or at least a pale, light-bodied lager inspired by it) is now brewed ubiquitously around the world. The classic versions are either bronzy-gold, full of Saaz, and off-dry with decoction-mashed richness (Bohemian Pils); or straw blonde, bone-dry, and crisply hop-bitter (German Pils). Using German Pils as a template we'll take a globetrotting approach to hops for our cold weather, slow-fermented pale lager.

Textbook German Pils makes use of noble hops like Hallertauer, Hersbrucker, Tettnanger, and Saaz. Low in alpha acid and cohumu-lone, these hop varieties all have a wonderful, delicate aroma and yield a very mild, easygoing bitterness, even when used at high rates in the kettle.

We're going to explore a slightly different paradigm with New Zealand varieties that share this noble ancestry: Motueka and Pacifica, which have Saaz and Mittelfruh parentage, respectively. These will add a layer of funky tropical fruit (which will be comfort-ing and familiar for IPA nerds) to the warm, earthy herbal character of the Old World landrace varieties. Regardless, emphasis in German Pils is on hop bitterness over hop flavor and aroma, so we'll keep hop additions away from the very end of the boil.

SHOPPING LIST

- 8 lbs. German Pils malt
- 8 oz. Weyermann Carafoam

- 1.75 oz. of your choice of NZ Motueka, NZ Pacifica (may be labeled as Pacific Hallertau), or a mix of both

- Wyeast 2124 Bohemian Lager or Wyeast 2042 Danish Lager

KEY POINTS FOR KEY PINTS

Pils malt, easy choice: Back in the day, when a beer was named for the town it was brewed in, the same town where the barley was also grown, ingredient choices were pretty simple. You still can't make a proper Pilsner without Pils malt, so opt for a good German malt like Weyermann or Best.

Yeast strain, harder choice: Wyeast 2124 Bohemian Lager will be a bit more user-friendly, with a more generous attitude towards fermentation temperature and a tendency to clarify a bit more readily. Wyeast 2042 Danish Lager will require a cooler basement or (better still) a temp-controlled fridge for primary and is a powdery son of a gun, but rewards us with terrific hop character, a snappy dry finish, and very low diacetyl production.

Fermentation, turns out it's important: Homebrewed lager is made or broken in fermentation, no matter how well-crafted the wort is. To focus on good fermentation, we'll keep our mash and boil regimen simple, and prepare a starter 24-48 hours prior to brewing.

BREWING

PREP
- Prepare a yeast starter, mill the grains, and heat strike water to approximately 163°F.

MASH & SPARGE
- **Mash rest:** Add all grains to strike water, mix to 149–151°F, and rest for 60–90 minutes. Collect and heat sparge water.
- **Mashout:** Heat it to 170°F for 5 minutes.
- Sparge and collect the wort in the boil kettle.

BOIL *(60 minutes)*
- **T-60:** 0.75 oz. hops (Motueka, Pacifica, or a blend.)
- **T-40:** 0.5 oz. of your choice hop.
- **T-20:** 0.5 oz. of your choice hop.
- **T-0:** Cool it, transfer to a sanitized fermentor, aerate well, and pitch yeast

FERMENTATION AND BEYOND
- **Primary fermentation:** Aim for around 48–50°F. Don't be alarmed by sulfury aromas—sulfur dioxide is a normal byproduct of many lager strains, and it will dissipate. If using 2124, plan a couple days of diacetyl rest. Allow the temperature to warm to about 58–60°F once CO_2 in the airlock slows and the krausen subsides. If using 2042, maintain a steady temp throughout since this strain tends to be a low diacetyl producer.
- **Lagering:** Store it at 35–40°F for 3–4 weeks. *Viel spass!*
- The beer will be ready to package roughly 6–8 weeks after brew day and will drink well as soon as carbonated. Pils is best fresh, so don't cellar it!

INTERNATIONAL INDIA BLACK LAGER

Targets: **OG:** 1.065, **IBU:** 40–45 (nominal), **SRM:** 30, **ABV:** 5.8%

Attempting to mansplain the stylistic DNA and categorical waypoints of this recipe will look to some (many?) like an exercise in cerevisiphilic insufferability. It's a black version of a hoppy pale ale, based on a misunderstood concept of what 19th century export beers were like, but which today bears even less resemblance to the first beers formulated around that fictionalized history—and it's fermented with a lager yeast.

But wait, there's more! It's going to use ingredients from four countries on three different continents (plus the Australian tectonic plate).

Do you even India Black Lager, bro?

As with the **Neck Tat That Says Evil Black IPA** (pg. 34), we want lots of roasted malt color and aroma without any roasted malt bitterness or astringency, along with a high level of pungent hop aroma and flavor. To achieve that, we'll revisit the technique of cold-steeping some de-bittered/de-husked roast malts, and gain most of our IBUs in a hop stand instead of during the boil.

To ensure that our India Black Lager remains obnoxiously cosmopolitan, we'll pluck the juiciest, grainiest, yeastiest brew-fruits of America, Chile, Germany, and New Zealand.

The base malts will be two-row plus a good slug of white wheat for texture; color will come from Bavarian Carafa and Perla Negra grown in the Chilean latitudes between the Atacama Desert and Antarctica.

Hop-wise, it's going to be a fruit basket—wild berry and bitter grapefruit pith from Comet, lime and peach from Wai-iti, a bit of apricot and papaya out of Idaho 7, while the tangerine quality of Mandarina Bavaria combined with the roasted malts might evoke a Terry's Chocolate Orange.

For fermentation, I'm calling for a steam-style California lager yeast for ease of use—that way we won't need to spend a sizable portion of the optimal hop-character window on VDK reduction or waiting for it to drop bright.

SHOPPING LIST

- 10 lbs. Rahr Premium Pilsner
- **Bag and mill separately:**
- 8 oz. Patagonia Perla Negra

- 1 lb. Rahr White Wheat malt

- 8 oz. Weyermann Carafa Type 3

- 2 oz. Comet
- 1 oz. Wai-iti

- 1 oz. Mandarina Bavaria
- 1 oz. Idaho 7

- Wyeast 2112 California Lager (or equivalent)

- Mesh bag for cold-steeping the roasted malts

KEY POINTS FOR KEY PINTS

Cold steeping: The Perla Negra and Carafa III will be cold-steeped just like cold press coffee. The resulting inky liquid added during the last few minutes of the boil will create a great chocolate-and-coffee roast malt character and deep color with minimal harshness.

Hop standing: Adding the lion's share of hops after killing the heat brings a big dose of fragrant hop oils and resin, which would otherwise be lost in the boil.

BREWING

24 HOURS PRIOR TO BREW DAY
- Make a yeast starter.
- Mill the Perla Negra and Carafa (keep it separate from the base malt). Place in the mesh bag and cold steep in 2–3 quarts of cold or room-temp brewing water for 24 hours.

PREP
- Mill the Pils and white wheat, then heat strike water to approximately 165°F.

MASH & SPARGE
- **Mash rest:** Add the Pils and white wheat to strike water, mix to 151–153°F, and rest for 60–90 minutes. Collect and heat sparge water.
- **Mashout:** Heat it to 170°F for 5 minutes.
- Sparge and collect the wort in the boil kettle.

BOIL *(60 minutes, while refraining from mainsplaining the IBL's stylistic DNA to anyone.)*
- **T-60:** Add 0.5 oz. Comet. Remove the bag from the steeping liquid—use a colander to let it drain and collect the liquid.
- **T-10:** Add the reserved cold steeping liquid.
- **T-0:** Hop stand! Turn off the burner, add 1.5 oz. Comet, 1 oz. Wai-iti, 1 oz. Mandarina Bavaria, and 1 oz. Idaho 7. Cover the kettle and let rest.
- **T+20:** Proceed with cooling the wort, transfer to a sanitized fermentor, aerate well, and pitch yeast.

FERMENTATION AND BEYOND
- **Primary fermentation:** Aim for a temperature around 60–62°F. The wort should be at or near terminal gravity within about 8–10 days.
- If you can, cool the finished beer to encourage the yeast to drop, allowing another week or two to condition, and then package. Enjoy this one fresh.

STERLING POUNDER MAIBOCK

Targets: **OG:** 1.067, **IBU:** 30, **SRM:** 6-8, **ABV:** 7.3%

Citizens, I submit to you that my fellow residents of the Upper Midwest are arguably better able to appreciate a good Maibock than anyone outside Germany, from whence this blonde scion of the lager family hails. We sit at a similar latitude, where the sun rises late and sets early during the winter, and the long hours of dark are compounded by cold temps and bleak skies for months on end. Before Seasonal Affective Disorder had a name, before vitamin D supplements and trips to Puerta Vallarta, there was Maibock.

Maibock is actually the youngster of the Bock family. What we now call Traditional (aka dunkel or dark) Bock has a pedigree stretching back many hundred years, at least to the days of the Hanseatic League. The paler Maibock (which you'll also find year-round under the name helles or blonde bock) had to wait for the advent of Pils malt in the mid-1800s to be born.

The beer will be golden, crisp and flowery, perhaps with a youthful tang of sulfur. Instead of Pils malt, some of the darker iterations of Maibock use part or all Vienna malt—orange instead of gold, toasty instead of flowery, a bit more rich than crisp. There's no substitute for the character a good German malt gives this style. I especially like Best Pils and any of the floor-malted offerings from Weyermann, but there are many good domestic options these days. Rahr Pils is great, or check out Briess's limited-release GoldPils if you can find it.

But whatever the color, the idea of a beer built to welcome the spring is good one. Maibock is brewed with a sunny color and relatively forward hop presence in anticipation of milder, greener days, but with a strong beer's alcoholic fortitude out of respect for a climate where the average last frost can fall pretty close to Memorial Day.

Honestly, we sons and daughters of the Northland need a good half-liter of cheering the hell up at that time of year.

SHOPPING LIST

- 11 lbs. of either Pils or Vienna malt (or a 50/50 mix!) Pils will make for a deep gold Maibock, Vienna will come out pale amber.
- 1 lb. German Munich malt
- 1 lb. Weyermann Carahell

- 2 oz. Sterling

- Your choice of Bavarian-style (or neutral ale) yeast—I'm using Wyeast 2206 Bavarian Lager

KEY POINTS FOR KEY PINTS

Malty isn't the same as sweet! We want our malt flavors toasty and doughy, not sickly sweet. Balance the malt with good attenuation through mash temp and yeast health.

In all things balance: German hops are traditional, but many of their American-bred descendants like Sterling perform very well here. If you go Old World—Hallertau, Saaz, or Tradition—adjust the amount for the lower alpha acid content. This recipe is hoppy for a Bavarian lager, that doesn't make it an IPA. 30 IBU will merely even out the scales.

Not your grandpa's lagering schedule: Warming basement temps at this time of year put the hurt on a traditional aging regimen. Choose a lager strain that won't throw a lot of sulfur, add a diacetyl rest at the end of primary, then lager for a shorter time at higher temp (say, 40°s instead of 30°s), and don't be afraid to hit it with finings.

Ale yeast workaround: If you don't feel like going full monty with a lager yeast, try a neutral or malty ale strain (1007 German Ale or 1056 American Ale) and keep fermentation cool—as close to 60°F as you can manage.

BREWING

PREP
- Make a yeast starter, mill the grains, heat strike water to approximately 165°F.

MASH & SPARGE
- **Mash rest:** Add grains to strike water, mix to 151–153°F, and rest for 60–90 minutes. Collect and heat sparge water.
- **Mashout:** Heat it to 170°F for 5 minutes.
- Sparge and collect the wort in the boil kettle.

BOIL *(60 minutes, while shaking your fist at the gray sky.)*
- **T-60:** 1 oz. Sterling.
- **T-15:** 1 oz. Sterling.
- **T-0:** Cool it, transfer to a sanitized fermentor, aerate well, and pitch yeast.

FERMENTATION AND BEYOND
- **Primary fermentation:** Aim for the low-to-mid-50s°F. When activity slows, allow the fermentor to warm up to about 60°F for a 2-3 day diacetyl rest, about 10–14 days total.
- Rack to a secondary fermentor and crash cool to lagering temps—no time to be delicate. Lager for 3–4 weeks (or longer, if time allows.) Fine as needed befor packaging.
- Given its ABV, this beer will keep well for many months in a cool, dark place.

BAD KARMA SCHWARZBIER

Targets: **OG:** 1.052, **IBU:** 28, **SRM:** 28, **ABV:** 5.3%

There's an old-school, perhaps old-fogeyish, line of thought that sees low-to-moderate alcohol dark beers as nourishing, health-giving, even feminine drinks. This thinking connects the milk stouts of the British Isles to the low-gravity dark lagers of the Czech Republic and runs right through the dark black lager of Germany—schwarzbier.

The town of Bad Köstritz, home of Köstritzer Schwarzbier since the 1500s, was a destination known for its mineral baths and "cure houses." Its native schwarzbier was a sweet, low-attenuated beer of only about 2 percent ABV—a relatively vitamin-rich and carb-tastic beverage for all the spa-going tourists (no wonder its reputation as a restorative drink for convalescents.) Modern brewing technology and stricter adherence to Reinheitsgebot have combined to make today's schwarzbier a more highly attenuated, standard-strength lager.

The defining ingredient of schwarzbier is de-husked roasted malt. The outer husk of the barley kernel contributes the astringent, puckering, "grippy" tannins. When the malt is kilned to a very dark color (300–500°L), those husk tannins contribute to the acrid, acidic quality of many porters and stouts.

But schwarzbier, like other Bavarian lagers, is all about the smooth. By separating the husks from the green malt prior to kilning, the maltster can create a very dark, intensely flavored roast malt without the aggressive French-roast coffee character of, say, roast barley, black patent, or chocolate malts. This leads to a luscious, rounded roast character that allows the rest of the ingredients step forward—the high percentage of rich, bready Munich malt and a balanced use of noble hops.

We want a lager yeast in the Bavarian family. A Czech lager strain could work in a pinch, although many throw off a level of fermentation compounds (diacetyl and the like) that would be okay in a Bohemian Pils but unwanted in a schwarzbier. Northern European and American lager strains will be too austere and hop-emphasizing for our purposes here. Bavarian lager strains will favor the malt, perhaps exhibit a little sulfuric edge, but remain clean and balanced.

SHOPPING LIST

- 5 lbs. German Munich malt (e.g., Weyermann, Schill, etc.)
- 4 lbs. German Pilsner malt   • 8 oz. Weyermann Carafa Special Type 3
- 4 oz. Weyermann CaraAroma

- 1.5 oz. Hallertau Mittelfruh

- A Bavarian-style lager strain of your choice—I'm going to use Wyeast 2206 Bavarian Lager.

KEY POINTS FOR KEY PINTS

Go German: To shine, this recipe needs some de-husked roast malt. Weyermann Carafa Special is readily available and authentic, and it comes in three different roast levels of increasing darkness. This recipe calls for Carafa Special Type 3, the darkest.

Think Bavarian: To me, a hallmark southern German beer is superb balance. They tend towards malty but are still drinkable and delicious. The hopping is judicious rather than exuberant but it's still there. If we spring for the imported ingredients, mind our mash and fermentation temps, and treat our yeast well, we'll be rewarded with a full-bodied lager that's still gluggable by the half-liter.

A yeast starter is your friend: Good lager requires lots of healthy yeast. Culture up a yeast starter prior to brew day to maximize yeast health and increase pitch rate.

Ale yeast workaround: Try a neutral or malty ale strain, such as 1007 German Ale or 1056 American Ale, and keep fermentation cool—as close to 60°F as you can manage. A yeast starter is still a good idea.

BREWING

PREP
- Mill the grains, then heat strike water to approximately 165°F.

MASH & SPARGE
- **Mash rest:** Add all grains to strike water, mix to 152–154°F, and rest for 60–90 minutes. Collect and heat sparge water.
- **Mashout:** Heat it to 170°F for 5 minutes.
- Sparge and collect the wort in the boil kettle.

BOIL *(60 minutes, while performing rigorous R&D on some Köstritzer.)*
- **T-60:** 1.25 oz. Hallertau Mittelfruh
- **T-15:** 0.25 oz. Hallertau Mittelfruh
- **T-0:** Cool it, transfer to a sanitized fermentor, aerate well, and pitch yeast.

FERMENTATION AND BEYOND
- **Primary fermentation:** Aim for a maximum temperature in the low-to-mid-50s°F. When activity begins to slow, allow the fermentor to warm up to approximately 60°F for a 2–3 day diacetyl rest. 10–14 days, total.
- Rack to secondary and cool to lagering temps—roughly 34–38°F—for 3 to 4 weeks.
- Package when clarity and flavor suit you. This schwarzbier will be ready to drink as soon as it's carbonated and will keep well for several months in a cool, dark place.

AULD PROCRASTINATOR IRISH-AMERICAN RED LAGER

Targets: **OG:** 1.050, **IBU:** 28, **SRM:** 12, **ABV:** 4.8%

Let's say you brewed the Ryed Irish Stout (pg. 82) and think you're all set for St. Patrick's Day. But let's further hypothesize that you were seized with a sudden panic ("not enough beer!") or visited by unexpected guests. In that case, let's crank out a batch of balanced, copper-colored smoothness and turn it over fast.

Let's start with a standard Irish ale grain bill, take some liberties with the hop schedule to better suit our 21st century American craft beer sensibilities, and then conduct fermentation with a lager yeast—a high-temperature "steam"-style lager yeast, to be exact. This isn't crazy—the most well-known American-brewed Irish red is actually a lager. For our batch, the steam-style yeast is going to give us (or your mooching March 17 guests, or whomever) that familiar clean lager-ish profile, plus help us out in the brewhouse with very high flocculation. Clear beer, quick.

A homebrewed Irish red starts with Irish malt (or at least a good UK variety like Maris Otter or Golden Promise). Some UK crystal malt will boost the round, sweet malty character. And that red color? Like Irish stout, it takes its hue from roasted barley—although in much smaller proportions—but still enough to impart a light coffee flavor and a dryness about the finish.

Like Shane MacGowan's teeth or the Millennium Falcon, it's not much to look at but it's got it where it counts: a solid British Isles grain roster, a New World hop load with nefarious intentions for this normally malt-forward style, and a California lager strain designed to produce malty and brilliantly-clear beers in a short amount of time. With modest bitterness, moderate gravity, and enough color and malt-hop character to help cover up the flavors of youth, this beer should be ready to package inside of two weeks. *Good craic.*

SHOPPING LIST

- 8 lbs. MCI Irish Stout Malt (or any nice UK pale malt)
- 12 oz. UK 55L crystal malt
- 3 oz. roasted barley

- 1 oz. Palisade
- 0.5 to 1 oz. Glacier, or more Palisade

- Your choice of a "steam"-style California lager yeast—I'm using Wyeast 2112 California lager

KEY POINTS FOR KEY PINTS

Choose your own hop adventure: We'll use some finishing hops in this recipe, but you decide which kind and how much. Glacier and Palisade are both new-school American varieties, but with a slightly fruity, earthy, sweet-candy character that, to my nose, echo the high notes of some European hops and can play nice with Old World beer styles. Pick one (or blend them!) and decide on a quantity—a half-ounce will give a subtle undertone that meshes with the malt and roast flavors, a full ounce will stand out more.

Mash low for good attenuation: Being an easy-drinking beer means no sickly-sweet finish from a high final gravity, but Cali lager strains typically don't attenuate like overachievers. To counteract that, we'll mash a little on the low side to encourage more beta-amylase activity and a more fermentable wort.

Yeast starter for fast turnaround: In the interest of speed, make a starter before brew day to minimize the lag time between pitching and fermentation.

BREWING

PREP
- Mill the grains, then heat strike water to approximately 162°F.

MASH & SPARGE
- **Mash rest:** Add grains to strike water, mix to 149-150°F, and rest for 60–90 minutes. Collect and heat sparge water.
- **Mashout:** Heat it to 170°F for 5 minutes.
- Sparge and collect the wort in the boil kettle.

BOIL *(60 minutes)*
- **T-60:** 1 oz. Palisade.
- **T-15:** 0.5 to 1 oz. of your finishing hops (Glacier or Palisade.)
- **T-0:** Cool it, transfer to a sanitized fermentor, aerate, and pitch yeast.

FERMENTATION AND BEYOND
- **Primary fermentation:** 7–10 days, with a maximum fermentation temp in the mid-60s°F.
- After FG is reached, continue to rest in the primary for a couple-three more days to allow the beer to clarify, then package.
- The beer is ready to drink as soon as it's carbonated. Assuming it survives the 17th, it should stay sound long enough to reprise with a corned beef sandwich throughout the spring.

ANHYZER KING AMERICAN LITE LAGER

Targets: **OG:** 1.036, **IBU:** 10-12, **SRM:** 2.5, **ABV:** 3.5%

Light ("Lite") American lager is a fascinating thing. It's reviled as the antithesis of craft beer, but it's an undeniably crushable paragon of the "sessionability" to which many craft brewers aspire.

Reviled, because "lite" beers are the provenance of industrial-scale breweries owned by multinational conglomerates. Also reviled because they represent an extinction event in American beer—a loss of the geographic and stylistic diversity of the 18th and 19th centuries. Regional styles and small brewers were herded via Prohibition and consolidation into a choke point and disappeared, replaced on fluorescent-lit 20th century supermarket shelves with a ubiquitous and inoffensive pale yellow lager.

How much more delicious it becomes, then, to co-opt the beer of the conquerors. Because let's be real: when brewers and drinkers talk about "session beers," they mean something that's low enough in alcohol to enable the imbiber to have a couple-four and still keep his or her wits. By those criteria, this style fits the bill. And while some marketing from the other side would have you believe that "fizzy yellow beer" is for wussies, maybe there shouldn't be a stigma attached to uncomplicated enjoyment of lightly-hopped, light-flavored beers.

Further real talk: these beers are hard as hell to brew well. It's a real challenge for a small brewer, home- or otherwise, to turn out a low-gravity adjunct lager with such delicate flavors and aromas—any issues with fermentation, sanitation, or other problems with the process will jump right out. Walking that tightrope is not for wussies.

Hail to the king, baby.

SHOPPING LIST

- 4.25 lbs. Rahr 6-Row

- 2.75 lbs. flaked rice

- 0.75 oz. Saaz

- Wyeast 2007 Pilsen Lager

KEY POINTS

Yeast health: In a beer where strong flavors are a fault and there are no color malts or strong hops to hide defects behind, we don't want any wack Sacch spitting mad VDKs and acetaldehyde. We will need a large pitch of healthy yeast and O$_2$ prior to inoculation.

Long & low mash: The high percentage of unmalted adjunct in the grist will benefit from a longer mash time. If you normally do a 60 minute mash, aim for 75-90 minutes for this batch. Additionally, a low mash temperature will help us achieve the high attenuation and vanishingly dry finish this style requires.

Macrosize it: If you have a big enough boiler (or can borrow a second one), double up and make a ten-gallon batch. You'll figure out something to do with the extra beer.

BREWING

PREP
- Make a starter culture 24-36 hours before brewing.
- Mill the grains, then heat strike water to approximately 159°F.

MASH & SPARGE
- **Mash rest:** Add all grains to strike water, mix to 146-148°F, and rest for 90 minutes. Collect and heat sparge water.
- **Mashout:** Heat it to 170°F for 5 minutes.
- Sparge and collect wort in boil kettle.

BOIL *(60 minutes)*
- **T-45:** 0.75 oz. Saaz.
- **T-0:** Cool the wort, transfer to a sanitized fermentor, aerate well, and pitch yeast.

FERMENTATION AND BEYOND
- **Primary fermentation:** 50-55°F for approximately 12-14 days. When activity begins to slow, warm to 60°F for an additional 2-3 days.
- **Secondary fermentation:** 34-38°F for 3-4 weeks.
- **Serving:** Frosty mug, blazing sun over boat dock, baseball game on radio.

SVĚTLÉ KVASNICOVÉ 10° PALE CZECH LAGER

Targets: **OG:** 1.041, **IBU:** 30, **SRM:** 3.3, **ABV:** 4.0%

Nobody drinks more beer, per capita, than the Czechs. At 142.6 liters per year in 2014, they easily edged out the professionals in Germany and almost doubled what Americans throw back in a year. And it's pretty safe to assume that a good percentage of those 142.6 annual liters consist of something not unlike this beer—an unfiltered blonde lager with lots of hops at a highly sessionable ABV.

This is quite a bit like the "premium" Bohemian Pilsners with which we're more familiar in the US, but in a more compact package: around two-thirds of the hop bitterness and topping out around 4 percent ABV. Like Bavarian Kellerbiers, they're often served unfiltered, relatively young, and on draft.

And they're beautifully, elementally simple. Pils malt, Saaz hops, and lager yeast are a classic formulation—the peanut butter and jelly of the lager-brewing world. With such a short shopping list for a beer of such modest stature, it's well worth sourcing really high-quality ingredients. This recipe calls for a floor-malted Czech Pilsner malt—the combination of Czech barley plus the oxygen-starved microenvironment of a floor maltings produces a malt with great depth of flavor that punches above its weight in a low-gravity wort. Spicy, herbal, and lovely, landrace Saaz hops are kinda mandatory for these beers, as is a Czech yeast that isn't quite as crisp or attenuative as most German and northern European lager strains.

SHOPPING LIST

 • 7.25 lbs. Weyermann Floor-malted Bohemian Pilsner

 • 2 oz. Czech Saaz

 • Your favorite Czech lager strain—Wyeast 2278, White Labs WLP800, or Omega OYL-101

KEY POINTS FOR KEY PINTS

Low-mineral water. Real talk: Pilsner Urquell has the same IBU value as Sierra Nevada Pale Ale, but it doesn't taste like it. This is in large part because of the extremely soft, low mineral water it's brewed with. It's why Czech lagers can be hopped to hell but still taste "soft" and rounded instead of sharply bitter. Consider blending in some reverse-osmosis water into your brewing liquor, or substituting it outright if your source water is hard.

Long boil: Pale Czech lagers pick up quite a bit of color and character (as well as increased hop utilization) in a prolonged boil—90 to 120 minutes is pretty standard.

Non-decoction option: Add 4-6 ounces of Melanoidin malt to the grist to make up for some of the flavor and color, and conduct a single infusion at 152°F for 60 minutes.

Tmavé (dark lager) option: Replace the Pils malt with Weyermann floor-malted Bohemian Dark malt, and add 6 ounces each of CaraAroma and Carafa Type 3.

BREWING

PREP
• Make a starter culture 24-36 hours before brew day.
• Mill the grains, then heat strike water to approximately 148°F.

MASH & SPARGE
• **Decoction mash:**
   135°F for 20 minutes, decoct approximately 8 liters thick mash.
   156°F for 30 minutes, decoct approximately 8 liters thick mash.
• **Mashout:** Heat it to 170°F for 5 minutes. Collect and heat sparge water.
• Sparge and collect wort in boil kettle.

BOIL *(90 minutes)*
• **T-90:** 1.5 oz. Saaz.
• **T-30:** 0.5 oz. Saaz.
• **T-0:** Cool the wort, transfer to a sanitized fermentor, aerate well, and pitch yeast.

FERMENTATION AND BEYOND
• **Primary fermentation:** 50-55°F for approximately 10-14 days. When activity begins to slow, warm to 60°F for an additional 2-3 days.
• **Secondary fermentation:** 34-38°F for 1-4 weeks.
• **Serving:** Half-liter mugs, deck of cards, backyard.

LAGERS

SCHWARZGERÄT NONCOMPLIANT BLACK DOPPELBOCK

Targets: **OG:** 1.072, **IBU:** 30, **SRM:** 36, **ABV:** 7.4%

After Germany's reunification, Neuzeller Kloster-Bräu, a brewer in the former GDR, was compelled to stop producing their schwarzbier because they backsweetened it with sugar syrup (sugar being a big no-no under the Reinheitsgebot.) After a ten-year legal battle they successfully challenged the centuries-old purity law and were able to resume production.

A dark sugar adjunct would be welcome, even necessary, in a strong stout or Belgian ale, but it's out of order in German brewing traditions. But we have the luxury of not needing to be in order. Some D-180 candi syrup, made from beets and dates, well help darken the wort, and heighten the chocolate and coffee notes to boot.

In that same spirit of taking the Reinheitsgebot as suggestion rather than rule, we're going to futz with a strong dark lager by making it a bit too dark and goosing it with some Belgian candi sugar. By incorporating these tweaks into an otherwise pretty straightforward doppelbock grist, we'll end up with a big, warming late winter specialty with an understated hop bite and suggestions of sweetened espresso and milk chocolate enveloped in the comforting embrace of a strong Bavarian beer.

Illustration by David Witt

LAGERS

SHOPPING LIST

- 11.5 lbs. Weyermann Munich
- 8 oz. Weyermann CaraAroma
- 10 oz. Weyermann CaraBohemian
- 4 oz. Weyermann Carafa Type 3

- 0.75 oz. German Magnum

- Wyeast 2124, White Labs WLP830, or Saflager W-34/70

- 8 oz. D-180 Candi Syrup

KEY POINTS FOR KEY PINTS

Compliant grains: Munich malt is the foundation of most dark Bavarian lager styles, supplying loads of malty, slightly toasty flavor. A mixture of small percentages of dark crystal and roasted malts brings in color and flavors of cocoa, bread, and dark fruit.

Noncompliant sugar: Substituting panela or jaggery for some or all of the candi syrup would be a nice further tweak, if so inclined.

Turn it up to 11: The steps given are for a regular old workaday infusion mash, but a double decoction mash will further intensify the malt colors and flavors.

Low and slow: Cold temps and high gravity make for a long, slow ferment—12-14 days is just a guideline, so be patient and give it time.

Street-legal version: If you don't feel like flouting the Reinheitsgebot, substitute 1-1.5 pounds more Munich malt for the candi syrup. Omitting the Carafa will bring the color back into the acceptable range—mahogany brown instead of black—for a traditional dark doppelbock.

BREWING

PREP
- Make a starter culture 24-36 hours before brew day.
- Mill the grains, then heat strike water to approximately 164°F

MASH & SPARGE
- **Mash rest:** Add all grains to mash, mix to 152°F, and rest for 60 minutes. Collect and heat sparge water.
- **Mashout:** Heat it to 170°F for 5 minutes.
- Sparge and collect wort in boil kettle.

BOIL *(60 minutes)*
- **T-45:** 0.75 oz. Magnum.
- **T-1:** 8 oz. D-180 candi syrup.
- **T-0:** Cool the wort, transfer to a sanitized fermentor, aerate well, and pitch yeast.

FERMENTATION AND BEYOND
- **Primary fermentation:** 50-55°F for approximately 12-14 days. When activity begins to slow, warm to 60°F for an additional 2-3 days.
- **Secondary fermentation:** 34-38°F for 8-12 weeks.
- **Serving:** 0.3 liter Willi Becher, fresh dark rye bread, melting snow.

MÜNCHNER WIESN

Targets: **OG:** 1.055, **IBU:** 25-26, **SRM:** 4.5, **ABV:** 5.6%

September, and thoughts turn to tuba solos in a big tent and coppery-orange lagers. But what's actually filling steins at the Oktoberfest in Munich is blonder than we may suspect—the modern Bavarian festbier stands in the gap between a classic Munich helles and a pale bock. They're paler, less malty and a bit drier than the amber Oktoberfest beers exported to the US.

Colloquially named for the meadow where Munich's O-fest is held (the Wiesn), the yardstick for a blonde festbier is beautiful malt flavor combined with downright crushability. That's a combo that can get you in trouble quickly if you're trying to keep pace with a Bavarian on an empty stomach, so make sure to prepare some Oktoberfesty snacks (like, say, whole oxen on a spit roast over an open fire) for when this beer is finished lagering.

SHOPPING LIST

- 9 lbs. Weyermann Barke Pilsner
- 4 oz. Weyermann Carahell
- 12 oz. Weyermann Munich

- 1.5 oz. German Select

- Your favorite classic Munich lager strain—Wyeast 2308, WLP860, or Omega OYL-114 would be good choices

KEY POINTS FOR KEY PINTS

Killer Pils malt: There really isn't a better base malt for this style than a Pils made from Barke barley. It's an heirloom variety grown in Bavaria, known for its pale color, high extract, and full body. On its own, the Weyermann Barke Pils does tend to produce a very light-colored wort, so we'll supplement with small fractions of Munich and pale crystal to boost the color slightly as well as add dimension to the malt flavors.

Attenuation: The miracle of Munich lagers is that it's no chore to finish a liter because they're so well attenuated (which is absolutely what we're going for here.) A highly attenuated beer finishes dry and crisp without a lot of sweetness or heaviness. Maltiness and sweetness aren't the same thing, and a low mash temp combined with good fermentation will keep them from being confused in the mug.

Noble hops: Even though this is definitely a malt-forward style, a hint of hop flavor is still welcome. We'll get there through a first-wort addition and a 20-minute addition. I've called for Select because they're so, so nice, but German Mittelfrüh, Tradition, or Czech Saaz would do well too.

BREWING

PREP
- Make a starter culture 24-36 hours before brew day.
- Mill the grains, then heat strike water to 162°F.

MASH & SPARGE
- **Mash rest:** Add all grains to strike water, mix to 150°F, and rest for 60 minutes. Collect and heat sparge water.
- **Mashout:** Heat it to 170°F for 5 minutes.
- Sparge and collect wort in boil kettle.
- Add 1.25 oz. Select hops to the boil kettle during the sparge, before the boil actually begins.

BOIL *(60 minutes)*
- **T-20:** 0.25 oz. Select.
- **T-0:** Cool the wort, transfer to a sanitized fermentor, aerate well, and pitch yeast.

FERMENTATION AND BEYOND
- **Primary fermentation:** 50-55°F for approximately 12-14 days. When activity begins to slow, warm to 60°F for an additional 2-3 days
- **Secondary fermentation:** 34-38°F for 4-8 weeks.
- **Serving:** 1 liter Maß, obatzda, and a picnic table under a shady tree.

CERVEZA MAS INTERESANTE DEL MUNDO

Targets: **OG:** 1.048, **IBU:** 16-18, **SRM:** 7, **ABV:** 4.8%

What would happen if you transplanted the dry-yet-malty amber lagers of Vienna to the Americas and rebuilt the bulk of them with some New World raw materials? Immigrant brewers of the 19th century found that out when they relocated to Mexico from Austria and brought their brewing traditions with them.

Those brewers from over a hundred years ago gave birth to a family of copper-colored lagers which, these days, are a mainstay of Cinco de Mayo parties north of the border. Unlike their Viennese ancestors, these international amber lagers are often brewed with adjuncts for color and flavor, and feature much lower hop character. Not that this is a bad thing when you're trying to bust open a piñata or maintain structural integrity on a tostada.

Illustration by David Witt

SHOPPING LIST

- 6 lbs. Rahr 2-Row
- 1 lb. flaked maize
- 1.5 lbs. Weyermann Vienna
- 6 oz. Patagonia Caramel 90L

- 1.25 oz. German Select

- Wyeast 2124, White Labs WLP830, or Saflager W-34/70

KEY POINTS FOR KEY PINTS

Dark caramel malt and corn: Where a continental Vienna lager would rely solely on its eponymous base malt for color and flavor, its descendants in the Americas make use of caramel malts and native unmalted adjuncts. Just a little bit of 90L malt will give us a pale amber wort with tones of toffee and dark fruit, while a modest inclusion of corn will de-escalate malt flavor and keep the body light.

The most interesting lager yeast in the world: The Weihenstephaner 34/70 is reportedly the most widely-used lager strain the world over, which puts it in the running for most-used beer yeast, period. It's attenuative, it emphasizes malt but doesn't bury hop character, and it's pretty easy to work with.

Fermentation for low flavor: As with many lagers, the compounds produced by stressed yeast cells or warm fermentation temps will stand out like a sore thumb. Propagating a yeast starter, thoroughly oxygenating the cooled wort before pitching yeast, and managing temps during primary fermentation will help produce a nice, clean flavor profile.

BREWING

PREP
- Make a starter culture 24-36 hours before brew day.
- Mill the grains, then heat strike water to approximately 164°F.

MASH & SPARGE
- **Mash:** 152°F for 60 minutes. Collect and heat sparge water.
- **Mashout:** 170°F for 5 minutes.
- Sparge and collect wort in boil kettle.

BOIL *(60 minutes)*
- **T-60:** 1 oz. Select.
- **T-15:** 0.25 oz. Select.
- **T-0:** Cool the wort, transfer to a sanitized fermentor, aerate well, and pitch yeast.

FERMENTATION AND BEYOND
- **Primary fermentation:** 50-55°F for approximately 12-14 days; when fermentation activity begins to slow, warm to 60°F for an additional 2-3 days.
- **Secondary fermentation:** 34-38°F for 3-4 weeks.
- **Serving:** Schooner, Los Lobos, piñata and/or tostadas.

ORANGE BLOSSOM HONEY TRIPEL

Targets: **OG:** 1.080, **IBU:** 30, **SRM:** 4.5, **ABV:** 9.2%

The Trappist abbey of Westmalle first brewed tripel in the early 20th century. Unlike its antecedent—dubbel, with its deep russet appearance and chewy, dark fruit character—tripel was formulated to emulate the light color and translucence of continental Pilsners, but at a much more deluxe gravity.

Some tripels use spices like coriander and orange peel to enhance their peppery, flowery bouquet. Others achieve complexity through yeast selection alone. Let's harness the power of orange blossom honey to imbue a tripel with a copacetic floral-citrus flavor.

Like the pale lagers that inspired it, tripel is brewed with Pilsner malt and low-alpha noble hops. The ale strains used by tripel brewers are characteristically spicy, estery, and phenolic with high attenuation and alcohol tolerance. And there's one more key ingredient—sugar.

Belgian brewers tout the "digestibility" in their strong beers. Compared to styles with similar OGs—doppelbock, barleywine, and wee heavy—tripel is downright dry, crisp, and highly drinkable despite its elevated ABV. Adding simple sugar to wort not only increases ABV, it also thins the body and mouthfeel and lowers the final gravity.

Our tripel will get dosed with honey not in the kettle, but in the fermentor. There are a couple good reasons for adding sugar post-krausen instead of to the boil for a beer like this:

The first and most important reason is to preserve aromatics. It's a waste to utilize an expensive and expressive sugar like single-source honey, only to have its character scrubbed out by heat, boiling, and the rapid evolution of CO_2 in the early stages of fermentation.

The second is to make sure the yeast consumes a large portion of the malt sugars first. Otherwise, they will metabolize the honey ahead of the more complex malt sugars, and as ABV rises, the yeast may weaken before attenuation is reached, leading to a syrupy-sweet tripel with a high FG. For a "highly digestible" tripel, let's encourage the yeast to get the hard work out of the way while they're still in peak condition.

SHOPPING LIST

- 12 lbs. Belgian Pilsner malt

- 3 oz. Saaz

- A liquid Trappist or abbey-style ale strain of your choice—I'm using Wyeast 3787 Trappist High Gravity Ale

- 2 lbs. orange blossom honey

KEY POINTS FOR KEY PINTS

Good yeast, lots of it: Like many Belgian styles, tripel is all about the yeast. Authentic Belgian and Trappist-style strains are readily available. Making a starter is non-optional today.

Nail polish remover is for hands, not beer: The alcohol in a well-brewed tripel is subtle and never harsh or solvent-like. Give the cooled wort plenty of O_2 prior to inoculation and mind your fermentation temperature. Too warm produces unpleasant fusels and higher alcohols, a common defect in homebrewed tripels. Consult the manufacturer specs for the recommended temperature range of your strain and err on the low side.

No orange blossom honey? Clover and basswood are my top substitutes.

Be ready for blow-off: Many Trappist-style strains are top-croppers, so have at least 33 percent headspace in your primary fermentor or just start with a blow-off hose right away.

BREWING

PREP
- Make a yeast starter, mill the grains, and heat strike water to approximately 158°F.

MASH & SPARGE
- **Mash rest:** Add all grains to strike water, mix to 148°F, and rest for 60–90 minutes. Collect and heat sparge water.
- **Mashout:** Heat it 170°F for 5 minutes.
- Sparge and collect the wort in the boil kettle.

BOIL *(60 minutes)*
- **T-60:** 2 oz. Saaz.
- **T-30:** 1 oz. Saaz.
- **T-0:** Cool it, transfer to a sanitized fermentor, aerate well, and pitch yeast.

FERMENTATION AND BEYOND
- **Primary fermentation:** Around 14 days, somewhere between 65–75°F.
- 2–3 days after fermentation starts in earnest (CO_2 through the airlock, krausen on the beer) add the honey. Make sure it's liquified and easily pourable, remove the stopper from the fermentor, and pour in the honey. Re-seal and swirl gently to mix. Expect renewed fermentation—it may be slower than before.
- Monitor the gravity, and don't rush it. We'd like a FG as close to 1.012 or so as possible.
- **Secondary fermentation:** A couple weeks of conditioning, then package.
- Bottle-conditioning is traditional for tripel, but no shame in putting this in a corny keg. Avoid oxygen pickup, store it cool and out of the light, and this beer will keep for years.

SCHRÖDINGER'S WEISSBIER

Targets: **OG:** 1.050, **IBU:** 12–15, **SRM:** 4.2, **ABV:** 5.0%

"The best songs will never gets sung/The best life never leaves your lungs."

Wilco was right: Everything exists in a quantum state of perfection as long as it remains only pure potential. A glimmer in the eye. An unfermented maltose molecule. It's only after we choose a fork in the road—an observable, fermentable one—that it collapses into A or B, this or that, banana or clove.

Traditional weissbier (aka hefeweizen) is a pale-ish, cloudy ale made from at least 50% malted wheat. The remainder of the grain is malted barley with most of that being pale, light Pils malt. Add some German hops, shoot for 5 percent ABV—pretty standard fare so far.

But it's the yeast that truly makes a weissbier. I'm calling for the most widely used strain in its native Bavaria, available at your LHBS as Wyeast 3068 Weihenstephan. Besides being uber-traditional, this weissbier is also an exploration of the mutability of beer yeast.

During fermentation, this strain produces the classic "clove" phenol (4-vinyl guaicol, or 4VG if you're nasty) and "banana" ester (isoamyl acetate) requisite of true weissbier. The amount and proportion of each is a chance for you get all Dr. Moreau with your yeast, tweaking and dialing the sensory profile to your exacting specifications.

For a banana-forward weissbier—think Hacker-Pschorr Weisse—try a single-temp infusion mash, a low pitch rate, a warm fermentation temp (mid 70s°F), and if possible a fermenting vessel that's wider than it is tall, for a shallow depth of liquid.

For a higher clove presence—like Schneider Weisse—we'll do a multi-temp mash that includes a ferulic acid rest, to liberate some 4VG precursors from the wheat. We will want to increase the amount of yeast pitched (with a starter, natch), aim for a cooler fermentation temp (low to mid 60s°F) and ferment in a taller, narrower vessel.

If you want to walk a middle path and balance out the ester and phenol character, pitch a healthy amount of yeast and ferment in the mid to upper 60s°F. Ready?

SHOPPING LIST

- 4.5 lbs. German wheat malt
- 1 lb. German Munich malt
- 3.5 lbs. German Pils malt
- Rice or oat hulls (optional)

- 1 oz. German noble variety (Hallertau, Hersbrucker, Tettnang, or Spalt)

- Wyeast 3068 Weihenstephan Wheat

KEY POINTS FOR KEY PINTS

Stuck mashes kill a party: Personally, I don't experience problems with runoff or lautering with a 50 percent wheat grist, but some rice or oat hulls in the mash is cheap insurance.

Multi-temp mashes are cool if you like 4VG: A ferulic acid rest at 111°F will enhance 4VG during fermentation—but the mash will still need to be brought up through protein and saccharification rests in this traditional regimen. Whether you use hot water infusions, direct heat, or decoctions to raise the mash temp, plan ahead!

Blowoff tubes are your friend: The Weihenstephan strain is a "top cropper." It needs 33 percent headspace, and will happily erupt right out of a six-gallon primary.

BREWING

TEAM ISOAMYL ACETATE HAMMOCK
PREP
- Don't make a yeast starter prior to brew day—one of the few times I'll say that.
- Heat strike water to about 165°F.

MASH & SPARGE
- Add all milled grains to strike water.
- **Mash rest:** 151–153°F for 60–90 minutes. Collect and heat sparge water.
- **Mashout:** Heat it to 170°F for 5 minutes.
- Sparge and collect the wort in the boil kettle.

BOIL *(60 minutes)*
- **T-60:** 1 oz. noble German hops.
- **T-0:** Cool it, transfer to a sanitized fermentor, aerate well, and pitch yeast.

FERMENTATION
- Aim for around 72–74°F.

TEAM 4VG (YOU NASTY)
PREP
- Make a yeast starter—overpitching suppresses isoamyl acetate, which allows the 4VG to stand out more.
- Heat strike water to about. 121°F.

MASH & SPARGE
- Add all milled grains to strike water.
- **Mash rest:** 111°F for 15 minutes. Collect and heat sparge water.
- Raise temp to 130°F, rest 30 minutes.
- Raise temp to 156°F, rest 15 minutes.
- **Mashout:** Heat it to 170°F for 5 minutes.
- Sparge and collect the wort in the boil kettle.

BOIL *(60 minutes)*
- **T-60:** 1 oz. noble German hops.
- **T-0:** Cool it, transfer to a sanitized fermentor, aerate well, and pitch yeast.

FERMENTATION
- Aim for around 64°F.

BEYOND FERMENTATION *(both schedules)*
- Primary fermentation should be complete within about 7–10 days, after which the beer can go straight into the bottle or keg. Weissbier is a beer of the moment—drink it as fresh as possible, as soon as it's carbonated.

SAISON CLASSIC

Targets: **OG:** 1.054, **IBU:** 30, **SRM:** 4.5, **ABV:** 6.0%

Saison is arguably the epitome of a "farmhouse beer." In the French-speaking Belgian province of Wallonia, self-sufficient farmsteads brewed their own ales during the cold months to keep their cellars stocked during the planting, growing, and harvesting seasons. They used a variety of cereal grains—barley, wheat, oats, spelt—and a range of botanicals, hence saison's locavore, agricultural heritage.

Mapping a saison on a spider chart makes it look on paper like the flavor explosion that it is in the glass: fruity, citric, spicy, earthy, musty, grainy, peppery, hoppy, herbal, bitter, tart, prickly with effervescence, perhaps funky or slightly sour from some non-*Saccharomyces* action. These yeast-derived impressions are prominent. There's no such thing as a boring (or adjective-deficient) saison.

There's incredible diversity under this single-word stylistic umbrella. But they all share a "rustic" quality, dryness (from high attenuation, hard water, or both), a high level of carbonation, and, most importantly, yeast-driven complexity.

Without the right strain, the "rustic" quality is lost. Fortunately, your LHBS has several (some of which include sour or wild bugs as part of a blend). The archetypal yeast comes from a hallmark saison brewery: Brasserie Dupont. In *Great Beers of Belgium*, author Michael Jackson relates a saying: "A brewer with the Dupont yeast is touched by God." It is justifiably famous for an immensely complex bouquet. It is also justifiably famous for being a finicky bastard.

European ingredients are traditional—Pils and Vienna malts for a base, Munich malt and perhaps the aforementioned wheat/oats/spelt/what-have-you in a supporting role, and maybe a small dose of simple sugar to ensure high attenuation and reinforce the dry finish.

Noble, low-alpha continental or English hop varieties are added throughout the boil (and sometimes dry-hopped). The use of herbs and spices is not required, but not unheard of either—coriander and grains of paradise are just two of many possibilities.

Having said all that, many of the "dank tropical fruit" hops now available from the Southern Hemisphere (Galaxy, Nelson Sauvin, Motueka, Wakatu) work nicely in a saison, especially its lighter, paler iterations.

SHOPPING LIST

- 5 lbs. Belgian Pilsner malt (or sub German Pils)
- 1 lb. wheat malt
- 4 lbs. Belgian Vienna malt (or sub German Vienna)

- 1.75 oz. East Kent Golding
- 0.75 oz. Styrian Golding

- Wyeast 3711 (or any saison strain or blend that suits your fancy.)

KEY POINTS FOR KEY PINTS

Mash low for high attenuation: In my book, there's no such thing as a too-dry saison. Chaptalizing the wort with a small percentage of table sugar or honey won't hurt either, but the 3711 strain should have no problem finishing work south of 1.010 on its own.

Touched by the Dupont yeast? Inquire at your LHBS for availability for the famous strain. It's a fantastic yeast that reliably produces a wonderful saison—if you can wait. It's notoriously slow to ferment out and known to freeze up in the middle of primary and then start again days later. The best approach is to overpitch with a big starter, give it plenty of O_2, ferment hot (above 80°F), and remain patient. It's made me wait before, but never let me down.

BREWING

PREP
- Make a yeast starter—especially critical if using the Dupont strain.
- Mill the grains, then heat strike water to approximately 156°F.

MASH & SPARGE
- **Mash rest:** Add all grains to strike water, mix to 148°F, and rest 60–90 minutes. Collect and heat sparge water.
- **Mashout:** Heat it to 170°F for 5 minutes.
- Sparge and collect the wort in the boil kettle.

BOIL *(60 minutes)*
- **T-60:** 1 oz. East Kent Golding.
- **T-15:** 0.5 oz. East Kent Golding and 0.5 oz Styrian Golding.
- **T-0:** Cool it, transfer to a sanitized fermentor, aerate well, and pitch yeast.

FERMENTATION AND BEYOND
- **Primary fermentation:** Aim for no lower than 70°F, and possibly even above 80°F—consult the yeast lab's specs. This should be completed in 7–30 days (remember, patience!)
- Rack to a secondary fermentor (if desired), and dose with the dry hops—0.25 oz. each East Kent Golding and Styrian Golding. Leave the beer in contact with the dry hops for 5 days (or to your taste), then rack and package. Aim for a high level of CO_2 in the keg or bottle, between 2 and 3 vols.
- Our saison will be ready to drink as soon as it's carbonated, but—since this was a style meant for laying down and keeping—it will continue to evolve in a cool cellar or fridge for many months.

SMOKE 'EM IF YOU GOT 'EM RAUCHWEIZEN

Targets: **OG:** 1.048, **IBU:** 15, **SRM:** 14.5, **ABV:** 5.3%

In his book *The Brewmaster's Table,* author and brewer Garrett Oliver lauds the versatility of Bavarian weissbier as a pairing companion for a wide range of dishes and cuisines. Its simultaneous sweetness, tartness, high effervescence, and host of yeast-derived flavors make it a good match for everything from brunch to spicy Indian or Thai curries. Dunkelweizen, a variant brewed with dark malts for deeper flavor and color, goes especially well with chocolaty Mexican *moles* or molasses-heavy barbecue sauce.

This information is especially valuable heading into outdoor-food season: Let's make a beer for barbecue and tacos.

Rauchweizen is a sub-subspecies of weissbier: a dunkelweizen brewed with a portion of beechwood-smoked malt. By German law, any member of the weissbier family must contain at least 50-percent malted wheat; but apart from that, the defining ingredient is the yeast.

The top-fermenting yeast used for weissbier and all its variants is a unique collection of little beasts. In the sexy and ever-changing microbial taxonomy scene, you may see its genus referred to as either *Saccharomyces* or *Torulaspora*, but you'll know it by the trail of its fermentation byproducts. The weissbier profile is dominated by spicy (cloves, nutmeg, vanilla) and fruity (banana, bubblegum, plum) aromas and flavors that are created by the yeast.

With dunkelweizen, the wheat malt is flanked by darker base and crystal malts for a darker color and a more intense caramel/bready/chocolate malt character to peek out from beneath the yeast flavors.

At least some of those darker base malts will traditionally be dried over a beechwood fire, which gives a warm, phenolic overtone— sweet and woodsy—to something reminiscent of ham or bacon, which is precisely where the magic is going to happen when we pour a big half-liter vase of the finished product next to plate of pulled shoulder or brisket.

SHOPPING LIST

- 5 lbs. wheat malt
- 4 oz. Weyermann CaraAroma
- 3.5 lbs. Weyermann (beechwood-smoked) Rauchmalt
- 3 oz. Weyermann Carafa Type 2

- 0.5 oz. German Tradition

- Your favorite weissbier/hefeweizen strain—I'm using Wyeast 3068 Weihenstephan Weizen.

KEY POINTS FOR KEY PINTS

Beechwood, not mesquite: When it's time to bust out the smoker for the season, I am a hickory-and-oak snob; not a huge mesquite fan. Similarly, I prefer the gentler, more traditional beechwood-smoked malt from Weyermann for rauchweizen. If you prefer to sub apple, cherry, oak, or mesquite-smoked malt, go for it, but it will change the character of the beer.

Clove, not banana: Again, a matter of personal preference, but I find the spicy byproducts of weissbier yeast work better with the smoked malt than the fruity byproducts. That means we'll try to foster the creation of clove over banana through a high pitch rate and cooler fermentation temperature. If so inclined, adding a ferulic acid rest at 111°F to your mash schedule wouldn't be a bad idea.

Blowoff tubes are definitely your friend: Weissbier yeast strains typically form a prolific krausen—a 5 gallon batch can easily escape a 6 gallon primary, so to avoid heartbreak and mess, plan on either using a large-diameter blowoff tube or an oversized fermenting vessel from the start.

BREWING

PREP
- Make a yeast starter, mill the grains, heat strike water to approximately 165°F.

MASH & SPARGE
- **Mash rest:** Add all grains to strike water, mix to 151–153°F, and rest for 60–90 minutes. Collect and heat sparge water.
- **Mashout:** Heat it to 170°F for 5 minutes.
- Sparge and collect the wort in the boil kettle.

BOIL *(60 minutes)*
- **T-60:** 0.5 oz. Tradition
- **T-0:** Cool it, transfer to a sanitized fermentor, aerate well, and pitch yeast.

FERMENTATION AND BEYOND
- **Primary fermentation:** Aim for a maximum temperature of 64–66°F to promote clove over banana character in the finished beer.
- When fermentation is complete, rack to a secondary (if desired) for a brief settling period, otherwise proceed to packaging.
- Like other members of the weissbier family, our rauchweizen drinks best fresh and will be ready for enjoyment as soon as it's carbonated.

LA GRANJA AGAVE AZACCA SAISON

Targets: **OG:** 1.056, **IBU:** 28–30, **SRM:** 6.5, **ABV:** 6.3%+

Agave tequilana is the plant responsible for pulque and tequila. It's also an adjunct sugar source. Here, it produces a non-traditional farmhouse ale with new school hops, and a mixed-culture fermentation.

We'll need a few things to breathe life into this brew. Specifically, a Pils and wheat malt grist with blue agave nectar/syrup added in the fermentor; Azacca hops, because they have a cool name; a mixture of Saccharomyces and Brettanomyces to chew it all up; and your finest mason jar or solo cup from which to enjoy the heady freshness of a young midsummer farmhouse ale con agave.

Blue agave nectar has a delicate floral quality combined with a really interesting undertone that reminds me of mesquite, or maybe even creosote. Like honey, agave nectar or syrup consists largely of simple sugar molecules (fructose in particular) and will ferment right out, with a net effect of thinning the mouthfeel. Also like honey, its flavor/aroma contribution can be very slight and easily removed or overshadowed; we'll try to preserve some aromatics by adding it to the fermentor instead of during the boil.

I didn't pick Azacca hops solely on the basis of its name (though I think we can all admit it makes for some nice alliteration.) But a big late addition of the dwarf hop variety formerly known as ADHA 483, now named after the Haitian god of agriculture, is also going to bring some welcome tropical pungency that will meld beautifully with the agave and the yeasts.

Speaking of yeasts—a blend of saison and Brett will achieve a combo of tropical fruit mixed with woodsy, peppery spice. By all means deviate as you like, but do use a nice, earthy, funky saison strain.

SHOPPING LIST

- 7 lbs. Rahr 2-Row
- 8 oz. 60°L crystal malt
- 1 lb. Rahr White Wheat malt

- 1 oz. Azacca

- Wyeast 3711 French Saison and 5112 Brett. bruxellensis (or your choice)

- 16 oz. blue agave nectar

KEY POINTS FOR KEY PINTS

Ferment warm: Regardless of your chosen strain, saison yeast and Brett alike generally enjoy heat, making this an ideal high-summer brewing project. Shrug off your swamp coolers and let the fermentor temperature free rise for maximum farmhouse phenols and esters.

Add agave nectar late, use a big primary: Adding the agave nectar post-boil will help its floral-mesquite qualities carry over into the finished beer. We'll add it directly to the fermentor 1–2 days after pitching. To help contain any renewed foaming during or after the addition, use an oversized bucket or carboy (or at least have a blowoff tube ready at hand.)

BREWING

PREP
- Make a yeast starter, mill the grains, Heat strike water to approximately 165°F.

MASH & SPARGE
- **Mash rest:** Add all grains to strike water, mix to 151–153°F, and rest for 60–90 minutes. Collect and heat sparge water.
- **Mashout:** Heat it to 170°F for 5 minutes.
- Sparge and collect the wort in the boil kettle.

BOIL *(60 minutes, while donning your finest Cuervo visor.)*
- **T-60:** 0.25 oz. Azacca.
- **T-5:** 0.75 oz. Azacca.
- **T-0:** Cool it, transfer to a sanitized fermentor, aerate well, and pitch yeast.

FERMENTATION AND BEYOND
- **Primary fermentation:** Aim for a maximim temperature of 75–85°F, and watch for krausen development.
- 1–2 days after pitching yeast, or once the krausen is high and CO_2 evolution is rapid, uncover the fermentor and pour in the agave nectar. Watch for foaming during renewed fermentation.
- After 2–4 weeks, fermentation should slow and gravity should be more or less stable (although the Brett may continue to work for a while), at which point La Granja will be ready to package and drink fresh. Extended bulk aging or cellaring will diminish the hop character but bring out increasing Brett character.

WHEAT & BELGIAN-STYLE

THUNDER DRAGON BELGO-BHUTANESE BLONDE

Targets: **OG:** 1.072, **IBU:** 24–26, **SRM:** 4, **ABV:** 7.1%

Let's bash together some disparate elements to make a global whole. Using a Belgian blonde ale for the superstructure, we'll mix in the nontraditional adjunct of red rice—the chief agricultural export of Bhutan, the Himalayan kingdom of the Thunder Dragon—and co-ferment with a sake yeast and a Belgian ale strain.

Belgian blonde ale is a modern category, developed to compete with mass-produced international pale lagers. As such, it's milder and cleaner than comparable styles like tripels and Belgian golden strong ales. The style guidelines call it "subtle but complex."

As with other strong Belgian ales, sugar adjuncts are often employed to boost gravity and ABV while lightening body. Our tweak will be to replace sucrose or dextrose with red rice, which will bring a nutty, sweet, perhaps slightly mineral-like quality to the ale, as well as a faint pink hue to the grist. The only catch: it may be hard to find without ordering it online. Jasmine, basmati, even brown, could stand in nicely for red rice. Barring that, use some good ol' flaked rice from the grain room at your LHBS.

Simultaneous co-fermentation with two different yeast strains will bring in some complementary complexity—the requisite spicy phenols and fruity esters from a Belgian strain, with earthy, floral undertones from a sake strain that will play up the rice portion of the grist.

This recipe is inspired by (but not a clone of) Hitachino Nest Red Rice Ale. Let's cut the shuck and jive, like the man says, and brew some unique beer.

SHOPPING LIST

- 10 lbs. Belgian Pilsner malt
- 8 oz. flaked barley

- 0.5 oz. Chinook

- Your favorite all-purpose Belgian ale strain—I'm using Wyeast 3522 Ardennes
- A sake yeast strain—like Wyeast 4134

- 2.5 lbs. Bhutanese red rice or Thai red cargo rice

KEY POINTS FOR KEY PINTS

Yeast starters, part one: "Subtle but complex" is the phrase that pays for Belgian blonde ale—we don't want to get punched in the face by loud fermentation byproducts. One way to mitigate ester formation is to limit the amount of yeast reproduction that happens in the fermentation. By starting out with a greater number of cells, fewer new cells are budded in the fermentor, ester production is suppressed, and everybody is happy.

Yeast starters, part two: Start the yeasts in two separate flasks. Propagating together saves a bit of time and cleanup, but propagating individually ensures that one strain doesn't completely overpower and out-populate the other before getting a crack at the wort.

Diastatic power: Although it provides flavor, color, and lots of talking points, the rice is dead weight, enzymatically speaking. We're relying on the Pilsner malt to complete conversion of its own native starches, plus all of those from the rice and flaked barley. Old malt can go "slack," losing its diastatic power to humidity and age, so spring for fresh grain and mill it as close to mash-in as possible.

BREWING

PREP
- Make two yeast starters prior to brew day (See: Key Points)
- On brew day, cook the rice before collecting strike water. Then mill the remaining grains and heat strike water to approximately 165°F.

MASH & SPARGE
- Add all grains plus the cooked rice to strike water.
- **Mash rest:** Mix to 151–153°F and rest for 60–90 minutes. Collect and heat sparge water.
- **Mashout:** Heat it to 170°F for 5 minutes.
- Sparge and collect the wort in the boil kettle.

BOIL *(60 minutes)*
- **T-60:** 0.5 oz. Chinook.
- **T-0:** Cool it, transfer to a sanitized fermentor, aerate well, and pitch yeast.

FERMENTATION AND BEYOND
- **Primary fermentation:** Aim for a pitching temperature in the mid-to-upper-60s°F and allow the temperature to rise. When activity subsides and gravity is stable, rack to a secondary fermentor for a few weeks of clarification and conditioning.
- Once clarified to your liking, proceed with packaging. This beer can be enjoyed fresh but will continue to improve and evolve for many months if stored in a cool, dark place.

WEIHNACHTSDOPPEL-WEIZENBOCK

Targets: **OG:** 1.072, **IBU:** 30, **SRM:** 11.1, **ABV:** 7.4%

Hefeweizen, meet bock. Bock, this is hefeweizen. "Oh, we've already met."

It's time to think about what you want for filling glasses at Yuletide gatherings and imbibing while hanging stockings with care. For your end-of-year homemade libation, I suggest a weizenbock: a rich, strong wheat beer built for cold, dark months.

Weizenbock's (VITE-zen-bock) combination of malts and yeast imbue it with a native spicy flavor and considerable ABV that will complement everything from clove-studded ham to fruitcake to pork crown roast. And its handsome russet color will perfectly match the ugly sweater you're wearing and you're not going to lose the contest this year, dammit.

My first taste of weizenbock was exemplary—a friend who was a fan of Schneider's Aventinus brought a bottle to share. I was jolted by the depth and complexity, and, being familiar only with more modest, standard-gravity hefeweizens and dunkelweizens, unprepared for the strength. Weizenbock is not a guzzler, citizens. The OG straddles the bock-doppelbock divide (1.064–1.090) with a fairly high FG (1.015–1.022) for at best an off-dry finish. Fat-bottom beers, you make the rockin' world go round.

Like any good doppelbock, weizenbock takes on color, intensity, and bready goodness from Munich and/or Vienna malts—high-kilned base malts commonly used in dark German beers. And like an authentic Suddeutsche hefe, weizenbock relies on a high percentage of malted wheat for a velvety texture and rising-yeast-dough flavor. Fermentation with a traditional hefeweizen yeast strain leaves the finished beer with aromatic high notes.

In the spirit of brewing beer at home for you and your family this holiday season, here's a version with a really long German name. This recipe isn't an Aventinus clone, but, like most other weizenbocks, it does owe an inspirational debt to the original.

SHOPPING LIST

- 6 lbs. Weyermann Floor-Malted Bohemian Dark (an heirloom version of Munich malt—check it out!)
- 6 lbs. Weyermann Floor-Malted Bohemian Wheat
- 6 oz. Weyermann CaraAroma
- A handful of oat or rice hulls (optional: this can help prevent a stuck sparge)

- 2 oz. German Tradition

- Wyeast 3068 Weihenstephan or White Labs WLP300 Hefeweizen

KEY POINTS FOR KEY PINTS

Malt showcase: It's for the holidays, so don't cut corners on the grain bill. Quality in, quality out, citizens. I like the floor-malted products from Weyermann for a beer like this.

A little bit of CaraAroma: This will enhance the dark fruit character and create a nice bass counterpoint to the spicy aromatic treble. An additional tiny amount of roast grain wouldn't go amiss, lending some light chocolate notes, but tradition demands we don't overdo the Carafa. Weizenbock shouldn't be roasty like a porter or stout. Although, this is your beer, so maybe go nuts.

No cloying: Even if a beer is big and malty, it shouldn't drink like a diabetic coma-inducing milkshake. This recipe calls for a fairly low mash rest to lean out the body, plus bitterness at the high end of the scale to balance the inherent sweetness of the beer.

Keep fermentation under 70°F: This will prevent the yeast character from becoming overpowering, and prevent the warming alcohol component of this strong beer from becoming harsh and solvent-like.

BREWING

PREP
- Make a yeast starter. Mill the grains, then heat strike water to approximately 165°F.

MASH & SPARGE
- **Mash rest:** Add grain to strike water and mix to 152°F, and rest for 60–90 minutes. (**Option:** If you have the time, mash tun space, and inclination, a more intensive weissbier mash schedule can be used: 115°F for 15 min., 129°F for 15 min., 148°F for 30 min., 156°F for 15 min.) While the mash rests, collect and heat sparge water.
- **Mashout:** Heat it to 170°F for 5 minutes.
- Sparge and collect the wort in the boil kettle.

BOIL *(60 minutes)*
- **T-60:** 2 oz. German Tradition.
- **T-0:** Cool it, transfer to a sanitized fermentor, aerate well, and pitch yeast.

FERMENTATION AND BEYOND
- **Primary fermentation:** 64-68°F for approximately 7–10 days.
- **Secondary fermentation:** Another 7–14 days conditioning.
- The beer should be ready to package after 3–4 weeks, and will start to hit its stride 6–8 weeks from brewing day. Stored cold and dark, it will drink well for months.

SUPER SIMPLE BELGIAN STRONG DARK

Targets: **OG:** 1.083, **IBU:** 24-26, **SRM:** 18, **ABV:** 9.0%

There's something truly alchemical about eliciting a wildly complex (and strong) beer out of a short list of simple ingredients. For the monks of Belgium's Trappist breweries, this has been their wheelhouse for centuries. Consider their strong dark ales—dubbel, quadrupel, abbey, or otherwise. Many classic formulations are simply pale base malt, dark sugar, hops, and yeast.

This recipe takes its cue from that tradition, parlaying a minimal 4-line shopping list into an age-worthy ale of process-driven complexity and high strength. Fermentation with a Trappist yeast strain, plus the slow biochemical work of time, add their own layers and show new facets. But pay close attention to how you treat your yeast, because the difference between a good Belgian dark strong ale and a bad one is made in fermentation.

Lots of happy yeast cells pitched at peak condition into a wort with plenty of oxygen will create appetizing fruity esters and peppery phenols buzzing above an ambrosial bowl flavored with rose-scented ethanol and chocolate-covered malt candy with an off-dry finish. Too few yeast cells, even if happy, in an O_2-poor wort will result in a lackluster tumbler of cloying gloop with overtones of Band-Aids and cruciferous flatulence.

This beer will reward yeast starters and thorough aeration right before adding yeast. So do it right, citizens.

SHOPPING LIST

 • 13.5 lbs. Belgian Pilsner malt

 • 1 oz. Perle

 • Wyeast 3787, White Labs WLP500, or your favorite Trappist ale strain

 • 2 lbs. Belgian D-90 Candi Syrup

KEY POINTS FOR KEY PINTS

Dark candi syrup: This is the secret sauce: an invert sugar (a stew of sucrose, glucose, and fructose, all of which are more readily assailable by yeast cells than sugars from barley) made from beets and/or sugarcane and cooked down to a dark color and viscous consistency. It will not only provide a significant boost to the gravity and ABV, but also its requisite deep color and complex flavors of burnt toffee, milk chocolate, and light roast coffee.

Pitching and fermentation temps: In a warm wort with so much sugar, it's easy for the levels of yeast esters and phenols to make the jump from pleasant to overbearing. To keep fermentation byproducts from running totally amok early on, pitch the yeast when the wort is a good bit cooler than the target fermentation temperature. The yeast will generate its own heat as it starts to go to work.

Pale and black variations: To make a blonde version of this beer, just switch out the dark candi syrup for a pale or clear candi syrup. These beers can display a little more hop character than their dark counterparts, so consider adding an additional ¼- to ½-ounce of Perle hops at around T-20 or T-15 for flavor. To make a Belgian imperial porter-like riff, use the darker D-180 candi syrup for even deeper color and more pronounced espresso and baking chocolate character.

BREWING

PREP
- Make a starter culture 24-36 hours before brew day.
- Mill the grains, then heat strike water to approximately 165°F.

MASH & SPARGE
- **Mash rest:** Add all grains to strike water, mix to 151-153°F, and rest for 60 minutes.
- **Mashout:** Heat it to 170°F for 5 minutes. Collect and heat sparge water.
- Sparge and collect wort in boil kettle.

BOIL *(60 minutes)*
- **T-60:** 1 oz. Perle.
- **T-0:** Add 2 lbs. candi syrup, then proceed with cooling the wort. Transfer to a sanitized fermentor, aerate well, and pitch yeast.

FERMENTATION AND BEYOND
- **Primary fermentation:** Pitch at 66-68°F, allow to rise to about 75°F over 7–10 days.
- **Secondary fermentation:** 66-68°F for 2-3 weeks.
- **Bottle conditioning:** 60-65°F for 4-6 weeks.
- **Serving:** Chalice or snifter, sleepy dog or cat, philosophical conversation.

HOPBURSTED BRETT SESSION IPA

Targets: **OG:** 1.044, **IBU:** 40–45, **SRM:** 3.1, **ABV:** 5.0%

Look at that name: we're just a bourbon barrel short of hitting all the buzzwords.

This project will be to twist a very hoppy, low alcohol, and easy-drinking ale with a *Brettanomyces* funk so mild and approachable that Bootsy Collins would find it disappointing.

Up until recently, *Brettanomyces* was regarded as a spoilage microbe in all but a few beer styles (lambics, Flemish reds, and oddities like Orval). But with skyrocketing interest in the sour, funky, and farmhouse-inflected sections of beer, Brett is enjoying a golden age.

Beer critic Michael Jackson described *Saccharomyces* as being like a dog, and *Brettanomyces* like a cat—Sacch will behave as expected, and try its best to please, whereas Brett will be more inclined to do its own thing. I am a dog person, and will leave out extending the analogy to litter boxes, but the fact is that even if it's not very biddable from a brewing perspective, Brett can make some damn exciting beers.

Compared to Sacch, the pace of Brett fermentation can be plodding, taking weeks or even months to finish up. But it's a thorough worker, capable of fermenting more complex sugar molecules than Sacch cells can handle, and leaving beers very dry and well attenuated.

There are many strains of Brett, each with their own characteristics and sensory profiles. The one we'll use here is a blend containing a Brett strain with a milder, more easygoing profile than its better-known cousins *B. bruxellensis* and *B. lambicus*. A high pitch rate will help minimize byproducts and enhance its mildness, bringing out flavors of pineapple, peach, and blueberry that will meld with dank, fruity hop varieties like Citra, El Dorado, or Australian Galaxy.

Which brings us to hopbursting. Adding all hop additions during the final minutes of the boil is an inefficient way to achieve bitterness but an awesome way to pack on dense hop aroma and flavor. We'll marry the tropical qualities of this Brett blend to a bowlful of new school hops, and it will taste very good—but your cat will still crap in your house.

SHOPPING LIST

- 7.5 lbs. Rahr 2-Row
- 8 oz. Weyermann Carafoam

- 3 oz. total of El Dorado, Galaxy, Citra, or a combination

- Omega Where Da Funk Blend OYL-210

KEY POINTS FOR KEY PINTS

Still a dog/Saccharomyces person? If you absolutely don't want to introduce Brett into your home brewery, sub in a nice, not-quite-neutral American type ale yeast (Wyeast 1272 would be good.)

BREWING

PREP
- Make a yeast starter.
- Mill the grains, then heat strike water to approximately 165°F.

MASH & SPARGE
- **Mash rest:** Add all grains to strike water, mix to 151–153°F, and rest for 60–90 minutes. Collect and heat sparge water.
- **Mashout:** Heat it to 170°F for 5 minutes.
- Sparge and collect the wort in the boil kettle.

BOIL *(60 minutes, while scratching your dog's ears, appreciative of not having to clean a litter box.)*
- **T-5:** Add the entire 3 oz. dose of hops.
- **T-0:** Cool it, transfer to a sanitized fermentor, aerate well, and pitch the Brett culture.

FERMENTATION AND BEYOND
- Aim for a fermentation temperature of 70–75°F. Watch the specific gravity rather than airlock, since Brett's slow and steady pace can make the bubbles (or lack thereof) deceptive.
- When the SG is stable and bright enough for your liking (this might take a few weeks), rack and package.
- Our session Brett IPA will be ready to drink as soon as it's carbonated; while the hop flavor will fade fairly quickly, the Brett character will continue to evolve with time.

WORD TO YOUR MOTHER BERLINER WEISSE

Targets: **OG:** 1.028, **IBU:** 5, **SRM:** 2.2, **ABV:** 3.0%

My mom doesn't like beer... except for Berliner weisse.

When my dad and I would homebrew, she would leave the house because of the smell. She is a wine drinker, and won't try any of our concoctions or, for that matter, any commercial beers. But one year, on a day trip from Hamburg to Berlin, mom was converted by what I imagine was a big-ass goldfish bowl full of that city's appellation-protected sour wheat beer.

What was it that made Ma Dawson a believer, where a parade of cream ales, fruit lambics, and blonde lagers had failed? It could have been that Berliner weisse is arguably the most wine-like of beers—Napoleon's troops called it "the Champagne of the north" for its highly effervescent and fruity nature. And while the acidic quality of Berliner weisse can be pronounced, it's not funky or aggressive like many other sour styles.

The engine that makes this German vehicle tear down the flavor autobahn is *Lactobacillus* bacteria and *Saccharomyces* yeast, fermenting side-by-side in a low-gravity, wheat-and-Pils wort. For our Sacch, we want a clean, neutral-profiled German ale yeast. The addition of Lacto metabolizes wort sugars into lactic acid—but not in the presence of hop acids, so an extremely low hop rate is mandatory to ensure proper souring. To help minimize bitterness, hops are usually added to the mash and the wort is boiled very briefly—if at all.

The lack of a wort-sterilizing boil, and the porosity of the wooden casks back in the day, leads to the belief that *Brettanomyces* are a traditional component of the Berliner weisse. If you choose to go that route, Brett can enhance the dryness and add a pleasant earthy note to the beer after extended aging.

This is short, sweet, and cheap, with no boiling and no secondary—consider doing a double batch, since Berliner weisse is light, dry, and tart, fun to drink and share, ages well, and your mom will probably like it.

So, for mothers everywhere, for summer, for the good times: Berliner weisse.

SHOPPING LIST

- 2.5 lbs. German Pilsner malt
- 2.5 lbs. German Wheat malt

- 1 oz. German Hallertau or Tettnang whole hops

- A sour ale blend for Berliner weisse like Wyeast 3191 or WLP630

KEY POINTS FOR KEY PINTS

Lacto: There are no shortcuts in this dojo. One cheat code from the Internet says to sub-stitute acid malt in the grist, or to spike the beer with food-grade lactic acid. Don't try this—Lacto fermentation flavor can't be faked.

Count IBUs on one hand: Lacto is extremely sensitive to hop acids, and tends to crap out (that's a scientific term) when IBU creeps into the double digits.

Boil if you feel like it: You really can just run the wort off from the mash tun, cool it, and proceed. If you feel the need to boil, keep it to no more than 15 minutes to prevent the wort from becoming too dark, or fully isomerize the alpha acids from the mash hops.

Keep DMS in check: The "creamed corn" aroma of dimethyl sulfide (DMS) is prevalent in Pils malt, but a defect in Berliner weisse. The minimum we can do is to cool the wort post mash (since boiling is optional.) If you have the capability for a single decoction mash, boil-ing a portion of the mash will help reduce the overall DMS level even more.

Bananas are for Cheerios: Keep away the hefeweizen strains! A blended culture already has Sacch and Lacto (and maybe Brett) in the proper proportions. With such a low-gravity wort, no starter will be needed.

BREWING

PREP
- Mill the grains. Collect and heat strike water to 145°F.

MASH & SPARGE
- **Mash rest:** Add all grains *and the hops* to strike water, mix to 133-134°F, and rest for 60 minutes.
- Raise the temperature via infusion, direct heat, or, ideally, using a small decoction, to 151-152°F for 15 minutes. Collect and heat sparge water.
- **Mashout:** Heat to 170°F for 5 minutes.
- Sparge and collect the wort in a sanitized bucket or spare kettle. Cool the wort.

FERMENTATION AND BEYOND
- Transfer to a sanitized fermentor, top up to 5 gallons, aerate well, and pitch yeast.
- **Primary fermentation:** Around 70°F to ensure good Lacto activity and rapid attenuation.
- Once the wort reaches FG (~1.007 should be about right using Wyeast 3191), go ahead and prime and bottle (or keg). Aim for a high carbonation level—we want it super-spritzy!
- Condition the bottles at fermentation temps for at least 4–6 weeks to allow sourness to develop. And don't be afraid to cocktail-ize this beer as Berliners do, adding a simple syrup of woodruff (check your LHBS), raspberry, or lemon (or spike it with schnapps!) This beer will continue to mature and gain complexity for many months after packaging.

MINNESOTA WEISSE

Targets: **OG:** 1.040, **IBU:** <10, **SRM:** 2.9, **ABV:** 4.2%

Let's bust out our kettle-souring regimen, citizens, for a beer inspired by Florida weisse—a riff on Berliner weisse that non-traditionally incorporates fruit (specifically tropical ones like guava, passionfruit, and dragon fruit) right in the fermentation, rather than added as a syrup in the glass when served.

To craft your own personal fruit signature on this weisse, the sky (and/or your farmers market or co-op) is the limit. Depending on the flavor of the chosen fruit, we'll need somewhere between 0.5–2 pounds per gallon. Something intense, like blackcurrants, needs only about 3–5 pounds for our batch. You'll need between 8–10 pounds of more delicate fruits, like raspberries and blueberries.

Making use of our local malts, hops, and fruit, it's time to give the world a Minnesota weisse.

SHOPPING LIST

- 3.5 lbs. Rahr Premium Pilsner
- 3.5 lbs. Rahr White Wheat malt

- 0.5 oz. your choice fruity/floral aroma hop variety

- Wyeast 5335 Lactobacillus, propagated in starter
- Safale US-05 or your choice of neutral ale strain

- Your choice of local/native fruit (0.5–2 lbs. per gallon)

KEY POINTS FOR KEY PINTS

Lacto starter: Kettle souring requires a big dose of bacteria, so we'll propagate a pack of *Lactobacillus* ahead of time. On brew day, mash and sparge as normal, followed by a cursory boil to sterilize, then cool. Pitch Lacto and ferment right in the boil kettle, keep it warm for a couple days, then boil again, add hops, and so on.

Hop choices: Local or homegrown hops are in keeping with the ethos of this recipe. If you have Cascade, Centennial, or anything from the Hallertau family growing in your yard, this would be a good place to use them. Vic Secret, Galaxy, Callista, or Wai-iti are decidedly non-local, but would be really nice for this beer.

BREWING

PREP *(1–2 days before brew day)*
- Prepare a *Lactobacillus* starter using 1 liter of water and 4 ounces plain light DME. Cool to approximately 100°F and inoculate with the 5335 Lactobacillus. Incubate at a very warm temperature (85–100°F) without stirring or agitation.
- Clean the fruit well, discarding any bruised or rotten pieces. Place the cleaned fruit in a freezer-safe bag, then put in the freezer until brew day.

PREP *(On brew day)*
- Mill the grains, then heat strike water to approximately 163°F.

MASH & SPARGE
- **Mash rest:** Add all grains to strike water, mix to 150–152°F, and rest for 60–90 minutes. Collect and heat sparge water.
- **Mashout:** Heat it to 170°F for 5 minutes.
- Sparge and collect the wort in the boil kettle.

KETTLE SOURING
- Use a boil kettle that has a well-fitted lid. Bring the wort to a boil for a couple minutes to sterilize, then allow to cool—you can use an immersion chiller if you like, or just let it cool passively with ambient temps (don't worry about DMS formation at this point—the wort will be boiled again).
- Once the wort temp is below 120°F, inoculate with the entire Lacto starter and cover the kettle with the lid. (If you want to go all-out, flush the headspace of the kettle with CO_2.)
- Allow Lacto to ferment 1–3 days. Do not oxygenate or aerate, and maintain a fermentation temp of 80°F or above. All other things equal, the bacteria will work faster at warmer temps, up to about 120°F, in an anaerobic environment.
- Once the wort has soured to your liking (a simple sensory evaluation of the sour wort will be enough), proceed to the main boil.

MAIN BOIL *(60 minutes)*
- **T-0:** Kill the heat, add 0.5 oz. of your selected hops, and let steep.
- **T+20:** Cool it!

FERMENTATION AND BEYOND
- Remove the frozen fruit from the freezer and dump into an empty, sanitized wide-mouthed fermenting vessel (at least 6 gallons—bigger may be better, depending on how much fruit you're using.)
- Transfer the cooled wort onto the fruit in the sanitized fermentor, aerate well, and pitch yeast.
- Depending on the yeast strain being used, aim for a maximum fermentation temp in the low-to-mid-60s°F.
- When gravity is stable and the beer is sufficiently clear (the fruit will contribute some amount of haze), siphon off the fruit, and proceed with packaging.
- Don't delay gratification—enjoy immediately.

OUD BRUIN PROVISIONAL SOUR BELGIAN BROWN

Targets: **OG:** 1.068, **IBU:** 13–15, **SRM:** 23, **ABV:** 7.5%

Summer is entirely the wrong weather to drink something strong, dark, and malty. But plan ahead, because six months from now, we might want a beer exactly like that. And unless you have refrigeration, it's too hot to ferment a nice pale lager—but it's damn near perfect for fermenting a sour Belgian ale.

This sour brown ale—a provision-strength Flanders brown, aka Oud Bruin—is native to the eastern portion of Flanders in Belgium. It's a bit of a relic and a living window into brewing history: dark brown in color (as all beers were, just a couple centuries ago), brewed on the strong side for laying down in the cellar, and fermented with a mixed-culture of ale yeast and bacteria that created increasing sourness as the beer aged.

Today, these beers are less well-known in the US than their sour red ale cousins (like Rodenbach or Cuvée des Jacobins). Oud Bruin is maltier, softer, unoaked, and less tart than those ales—a little more substantial, a bit less quenching and zippy.

Like other Belgians, Flanders brown ale is built on a base of continental malts—mainly Pils, often with a little unmalted flaked maize as an adjunct. Caramel and roasted malts (and the color and flavor they contribute) are crucial in differentiating Oud Bruin from other members of the sour ale family, creating a deep red-brown color and rich, complex malt character.

But the engine that hauls this flavor train into Mouth Station are the microbes. A *Saccharomyces* ale strain plus lactic acid bacteria (usually *Lactobacillus*) are mandatory; *Brettanomyces* isn't, which is another differentiator of Oud Bruin, and a reason the overall profile of a Flanders brown is "softer" than that of other Belgian sour ales.

The final effect is a chalice or goblet (this ain't a shaker pint beer, citizens) capped with tan lace holding down aromatic overtones of caramel, dark fruit, chocolate, and brown sugar. While young, the fermentation character will be vaguely funky and perhaps phenolic, but with time it segues into beautifully tart and slightly tangy, with a well-attenuated finish.

SHOPPING LIST

- 6.75 lbs. Belgian Pils malt
- 8 oz. Belgian CaraRuby
- 8 oz. flaked maize
- 4 oz. Belgian Special B

- 4 lbs. Vienna malt
- 8 oz. 80°L crystal malt
- 3 oz. chocolate malt

- 1.25 oz. Hallertau

- A blended liquid yeast culture for Flemish-style sour ales—I'm using Wyeast 3763 Roeselare Blend

- 5–10 lbs. of fresh fruit—tart cherries or raspberries (see Key Points)

KEY POINTS FOR KEY PINTS

Low IBUs: Lactic acid bacteria are sensitive to hop acids, and we don't want hop bitterness to clash with the fantastic malt profile we're building. We'll be able to take off our Tevas and count the IBUs for this batch on our fingers and toes, and still have some digits left over.

Keep it warm: *Lactobacillus* love warm fermentation temps but hate high alcohol levels— let's encourage acid production early on in the fermentation, before the bacteria become inhibited by rising alcohol levels. For the blend I'm using, a fermentation temp in the low-to-mid-80s°F will strike a happy medium between bacteria and brewer's yeast.

Variations with fruit: To go this route, plan on a secondary fermentation in a bucket or wide-mouth carboy to make addition and clean-up easier. Blanch the fruit briefly in boiling water, then freeze until ready to use. Once fermentation slows, put the frozen fruit into the sanitized fermentor, then siphon the young beer in on top of it.

BREWING

PREP
- Mill the grains and heat strike water to approximately 165°F.

MASH & SPARGE
- **Mash rest:** Add all grains to strike water, mix to 151–153°F, and rest 60–90 minutes. Collect and heat sparge water.
- **Mashout:** Heat it to 170°F for 5 minutes.
- Sparge and collect the wort in the boil kettle.

BOIL *(60 minutes)*
- **T-30:** Add 1.25 oz. Hallertau
- **T-0:** Cool it, transfer to a sanitized fermentor, aerate well, and pitch yeast.

FERMENTATION AND BEYOND
- Aim for a fermentation temperature of 80-85°F to encourage Lacto activity.
- Rack to a secondary fermentor once the beer reaches terminal gravity (around 1.010–1.015, depending on your yeast). Condition at a warm temp in secondary until the flavor, acidity, and character of any optional fruit additions are to your liking, then package.
- This sour brown will take at least several months to fully develop, and will continue evolving for up to a year or two in your cellar.

VELVET UNTERBAHN KETTLE-SOURED GOSE

Targets: **OG:** 1.048, **IBU:** ~7, **SRM:** 3.3, **ABV:** 4.8%

Let's brew a traditional Gose by way of a modern souring regimen. Since long preambles are for single-strain fermentations, let's dig right in.

Gose is a top-fermented sour wheat beer flavored with coriander and salt. The style is reputed to have originated in the northern German town of Goslar, where mineral-rich aquifers naturally yielded slightly saline water, but achieved the apex of its popularity in Leipzig. It was quite the rage in Saxony for a couple hundred years, but fell into obscurity after WWII and eventually went extinct for a few decades. In 1995, it was revived commercially in a Leipzig train station-turned-brewhouse, and craft-brewed versions can now be found around the U.S.

Like Berliner weisse, Gose is brewed with a large percentage of malted wheat, hopped very sparingly, and soured by a *Lactobacillus* fermentation. Where it diverges is in its typically higher gravity (compared to ballpark OG 1.030 for Berliner weisse) and the use of coriander and salt as flavorings.

SHOPPING LIST

- 4 lbs. Weyermann Pilsner
- 8 oz. Weyermann Acidulated Malt
- 4 lbs. Weyermann Pale Wheat

- 0.5 oz. your choice of a classic continental low-alpha noble hop (Hallertauer, Hersbrucker, Tettnang, Saaz, etc.)

- Wyeast 5335 Lactobacillus
- Your choice of a clean German ale strain (Wyeast 1007 or Safale K-97 would be good here)

- 0.5 oz. sea salt
- 0.5 oz. whole coriander

KEY POINTS FOR KEY PINTS

Why kettle sour? It usually sours a beer faster than co-inoculating, and it eliminates any risk of cross-contamination. Since Lacto and Sacch are added individually, fermentation conditions can be optimized sequentially rather than splitting the difference. Then, the Lacto are destroyed in the boil before the wort reaches your fermentor or bottling gear.

Our friend Lactobacillus: It's anaerobic, thermophilic, inhibited by isomerized hop acids, and mainly homofermentive—so it likes hot fermentation temperatures, hates O_2 and hops, and should reduce pH rather than SG.

Source good coriander and grind it right before use: We want lemony and zingy, not vegetal/celery/ham from old, stale seeds. Consult your premiere local spice emporium.

BREWING

PREP *(1–2 days before brew day)*
* Prepare a Lacto starter: 1 liter of water, 4 oz. DME. Incubate at a very warm temperature (85–100°F) without stirring or agitation.

PREP *(on brew day)*
* Mill the grains and heat strike water to approximately 165°F.

MASH & SPARGE
* **Mash rest:** Add all grains to strike water, mix to 151–153°F, and rest 60–90 minutes. Collect and heat sparge water.
* **Mashout:** Heat it to 170°F for 5 minutes.
* Sparge and collect the wort in the boil kettle.

KETTLE SOURING
* Use a boil kettle with a well-fitted lid. Bring the wort to a boil for a couple minutes to sterilize, then allow to cool. Use an immersion chiller or just let it cool passively with ambient temps. Don't worry about DMS formation—the wort will be boiled again.
* Once the wort is below 120°F, inoculate with the entire Lacto starter and cover the kettle with the lid. (If you want to go all-out, flush the headspace of the kettle with CO_2.)
* Allow Lacto to ferment 1–3 days. Do not oxygenate or aerate, and maintain a fermentation temp of 80°F or above—all other things equal, the bacteria will work faster at warmer temps, up to about 120°F, in an anaerobic environment.
* Once the wort has soured to your liking (a simple sensory evaluation of the sour wort will be enough), proceed to the main boil.

MAIN BOIL *(60 minutes, while humming along to "White Light/White Heat.")*
* **T-60**: 0.5 oz. of your selected noble hops. Grind the whole coriander seeds.
* **T-5:** Add ground coriander and sea salt.
* **T-0:** Cool it, transfer to a sanitized fermentor, aerate well, and pitch yeast.

FERMENTATION AND BEYOND
* **Primary Fermentation:** Depending on the yeast strain being used, aim for a maximum temperature in the low-to-mid-60s°F.
* When gravity is stable and the beer is sufficiently clear (some haze is accepted and expected for this style), proceed with packaging.
* Our kettle-soured Gose will show best while fresh—why would you sleep on this tart, refreshing little gem while spring is in the world?

WYLD CYDER

Targets: **OG**: variable, depending on harvest—let's plan for 1.045–1.055, **ABV:** ~5.0%

There was an apocryphal frost centuries ago in Hessen, Germany that wiped out that year's grape crop. The distraught wine-makers turned to apples and they haven't looked back since. That region is now the heartland of *apfelmost*—a hard cider, fermented with the naturally occurring microbes on the fruit and extant from year to year on the presses or in the barrels of the cider house.

Meanwhile, in Asturias and the Basque region of northern Spain, the beverage of choice for the last several centuries hasn't been Rioja wine but sidra, produced from native apple varieties and also fermented spontaneously with the wild yeasts on the fruit. Other cidermaking traditions rely on wild yeast to power the ferment: the keeved and slow-fermented cidres of Normawndy, and the powerful, funky, and heady English West Country ciders made from bitter apple varieties.

Taking a cue from these disparate traditions, this project is an adventure in wild cider (or, with apologies to Bill and Ted, WYLD CYDER).

It's unfiltered and acidic, complex and musty; funky up front and whooshing to a palate-scouring dry finish. Fans of gueuze and saison will find a lot to like here, while drinkers of much sweeter mass-market hard ciders are in for a Timothy Leary-grade mind expansion.

Many wild ciders are produced from heirloom or landrace cider (not table) apple varieties. But many little farmhouse operations would have used whatever they had on hand, so there's no reason not to pick up whatever your local orchard is throwing down.

The alcohol content of naturally-fermented ciders varies with the sugar content of the apples (in keeping with the precepts of non-interference, these wild ciders are not supplemented with any exogenous sugars), but usually clock in at 4–6 percent ABV.

SHOPPING LIST

If using fresh fruit and spontaneous fermentation:
- 5 gallons fresh, unpasteurized apple juice
- A pack of yeast for backup—see Key Points.

If using pasteurized or store-bought juice and lab yeast:
- 5 gallons preservative-free natural apple juice
- Your choice of yeast

KEY POINTS FOR KEY PINTS

G-g-gotta be fresh: Source unpasteurized juice with no sulfites or other preservatives from a cider mill, or grind and press your own apples. The untreated fruit will contain a bolus of native microbes that we'll harness to turn the juice into hard cider.

Don't kill the critters: Modern protocol would be to sulfite the freshly-pressed juice to nuke the wild yeasts from orbit and give the lab-cultured yeast a blank slate. Can't do this with a spontaneous fermentation, so leave the Campden tablets in the drawer.

Don't necessarily g-g-gotta be fresh: If fresh-pressed juice isn't an option, just use store-bought juice (preservative-free). You will, however, need to add your own yeast. To approximate a wild fermentation, consider a commercial mixed culture—Wyeast 3763 Roeselare, or a farmhouse or lambic blend (e.g., Wy3278, WLP670) would be good options.

Have a backup plan: If the juice isn't fermenting on its own after 48–72 hours, we'll need to add yeast, make sure you have a spare pack on hand.

Cool temp for more aromatics: Traditionally, cider would be fermented at harvest time in mild ambient temperatures. Keeping it around 60°F suppresses the rate of fermentation and therefore how much of the delicate fruit aromatics get carried out of our beverage along with CO_2 gas.

BREWING

SPONTANEOUS PROGRAM
- Rack the fresh juice into a sanitized fermentor; record the SG, then cover loosely with sanitized foil or an airlock, adjust to around 60°F. Let nature take its course.

STORE-BOUGHT JUICE/NON-FUNKY PROGRAM
- Decant the juice into a sanitized fermentor. Record the SG, then cover loosely with sanitized foil or an airlock, adjust to around 60°F, and add yeast.

FERMENTATION AND BEYOND
- Wild fermentations (or fermentations with a lab-mixed culture) can be very slow affairs, so remain patient. Once gravity is stable and flavor is to your liking (acidity and dryness tend to increase with time), rack to secondary.
- Allow to settle and clarify in secondary for a few weeks or months. You can more-or-less stabilize the flavor via cold storage (microbes will go dormant below about 40–45°F) or a dose of sulfite (to inhibit or kill the microbes.)
- Package once clarified to your liking. Many traditional wild ciders are served still, but kegging will make it easy to serve sparkling. If you bottle a non-sulfite product, use crown- or cork-and-cage beer bottles to accommodate any pressure that may develop.

IRISH HUNTER PORTER WITH BRETT

Targets: **OG:** 1.060, **IBU:** 55–60, **SRM:** 23, **ABV:** 6.5%

Now for a batch of historical-inspired porter with a mixed-fermentation and a bit of choose-your-own-adventure. Snug down your tweed caps and prepare to shock some delicate Victorian sensibilities.

Porter from the 19th century did not joke around—original gravities were much higher than the wartime and postwar 20th century versions of the same beers. Similarly, the hop rates were high and the beers were bitter, not hoppy (see: **Throwback IPA**, pg. 38.)

This is going to be a simple beer, ingredients-wise: two malts, a single hop variety. It's patterned after 19th century Irish porter, so we're calling for base malt from the Malting Company of Ireland. Back then, porters and stouts were all-malt, so we'll also use malted black patent (instead of unmalted roast barley, which didn't show up in Irish ale brewing until the 20th century. Also, no brown malt—that was a London porter thing.)

I'm calling for a single big bittering charge of East Kent Golding, but Fuggle would be authentic here, too. If you want to mix-n-match to hit the target IBU, non-UK varieties like Styrian Golding, Hallertau, or even Cluster would be appropriate (UK brewers made liberal use of imported hops in the later 1800s.) Just keep those 20th century hybrids like Challenger and Target out of our precious anachronistic illusion.

Finally, the decision-making: running or keeping? Publicans of the era would have served a beer this either as a running porter—fresh for immediate consumption and quick turnaround—or a keeping porter, aged for many months or more.

Drinking this beer young will highlight the tarry, French-roast quality of the black patent and the bittersweet admixture of malt, ale yeast, and hops. Time in secondary will mute the hop bitterness but also lean out the body, as well as add overtones of leather, smoke, funk, and ripe fruit. If you have a cask and beer engine, this would be a great beer to pour through it.

Fermentation with a blended culture of ale yeast and *Brettanomyces* will make both outcomes possible—in the same batch, if you want.

SHOPPING LIST

- 10 lbs. MCI Irish ale malt
- 8 oz. black patent malt

- 2.75 oz. East Kent Golding

- Omega OYL-211 Bit O' Funk Blend

KEY POINTS FOR KEY PINTS

Mash high for Brettanomyces: Brett consumes more complex sugars than Sacch can handle, so a dextrinous wort will give it fuel for the long haul. Plus, if serving a running porter, it'll make the bitterness and roastiness of the youthful beer more approachable.

Brett-phobic? Choose a single-strain Sacch—a clean-ish, dry-fermenting strain like 1028 or 1098 (but remember, you can eradicate Brett with a tight sanitation regimen.)

Make a Starter! Normally with a blended culture, I'd advise against a starter because it will shift the balance of microbes—the slower-working Brett population will shrink in proportion to the faster-acting Sacch. However, the Brett in these historic beers would have been largely incidental (e.g. via contact with a wooden tun or cask), and the high mash temp and extended aging will help offset the effects of the population change.

Bottle conditioning a keeping porter? Use strong bottles and use a lower-than-normal priming rate, as the Brett cells will continue to ferment dextrins after packaging.

BREWING

PREP
- Mill the grains, then heat strike water to approximately 170°F.

MASH & SPARGE
- **Mash rest:** Add all grains to strike water, mix to 156–158°F, and rest for 60–90 minutes. Collect and heat sparge water.
- **Mashout:** Heat it to 170°F for 5 minutes.
- Sparge and collect the wort in the boil kettle.

BOIL *(60 minutes)*
- **T-60:** 2.75 oz. East Kent Golding.
- **T-0:** Cool it, transfer to a sanitized fermentor, aerate well, and pitch yeast.

FERMENTATION AND BEYOND
- **Primary fermentation:** Aim for 68–72°F. When activity begins to slow, allow the fermentor to warm up to 72–74°F for a 2–3 day diacetyl rest.
- If doing a running porter, the beer can be packaged and served as soon as it's clear enough for your delicate Victorian sensibilities.
- If doing a keeping porter, rack to a secondary fermentor and hold for 3–12 months. The beer could be packaged at any point, but it may be advantageous to let the Brett fermentation run to completion under an airlock to avoid the risk of over-pressurizing a keg or bottles. Don't be alarmed if the beer forms a pellicle (a pale skin on the surface) during this aging period—that's the Brett doing its thing. The beer can be siphoned out from underneath it at racking time.

Illustration by David Witt

THIN WIT DUKE SOUR BELGIAN WHITE

Targets: **OG:** 1.049, **IBU:** <10, **SRM:** 3.5, **ABV:** 5.0%

Witbier is a wheat-based ale which originated in east-central Belgium. Its name literally means "white beer," although its actual color is more of a hazy straw gold. But it would have looked quite pallid next to the dark red-brown barley beers that were standard issue 400 years ago.

Because Belgium was a part of the Netherlands at the time, and because the Netherlands held various tropical colonies at that same time, a rather medieval use of exotic spices as beer flavoring is still a hallmark of witbier—especially coriander and the bitter peel of Curaçao oranges.

Witbier arose as a true farmhouse ale: brewed on the farm, for the farm, using grains from the farm. It incorporated malted and/or raw wheat along with pale malted barley, and often raw or malted oats. Historical documents indicate that witbier didn't usually have a pure-culture fermentation until sometime after the mid-20th century; prior to that, a mild to moderate sourness from lactic acid bacteria would have been a regular feature.

So we've already got a beer with multiple malted and raw grains, spices, plus sourness, and we haven't even gotten to the spicy, phenolic buzz of traditional witbier yeast strains. The hallmark of any great Belgian ale is the ability to bring all these disparate elements into balance in the glass, which gibes with our ultimate goal for this recipe as an approachably friendly, drinkable, quenching summertime tumbler-filler.

SHOPPING LIST

- 4 lbs. Belgian Pilsner malt
- 8 oz. flaked oats
- 4 lbs. Rahr White Wheat malt

- 0.75 oz. Hallertau Hersbrucker, or equivalent with very low alpha acid

- Wyeast 5335 Lactobacillus
- Your favorite Witbier strain—Wyeast 3944, WLP400, or equivalent

- 1 tablespoon whole coriander, freshly ground before use
- 1 tablespoon bitter Curaçao orange peel

KEY POINTS FOR KEY PINTS

Prep a starter for the Lacto: This'll help speed up the souring and eventual gratification.

Keep bitterness low and temp high: Most Lactobacillus is notoriously hop-sensitive and tends to conk out at levels greater than about 10 IBU. But one thing it loves is heat— keeping the initial fermentation at 80-90°F will promote its activity.

Multi-strain, multi-step fermentation: The Lacto starter culture will get first crack at the wort. Don't be alarmed if there is little change to the SG of the wort—at this point the main activity of the bacteria will be to produce acid, not alcohol. The witbier Saccharomyces strain will be added approximately a week later, once the lactic acid bacteria has done its souring.

BREWING

PREP
- Make a starter culture for the Lacto 4-7 days prior to brew day—use 2 oz. of DME in 1 liter of water, and incubate at 90-100°F.
- On brew day, mill the grains and heat strike water to approximately 163°F

MASH & SPARGE
- **Mash rest:** Add all grains to strike water, mix to 151-153°F, and rest for 60 minutes. Collect and heat sparge water.
- **Mashout:** Heat it to 170°F for 5 minutes.
- Sparge and collect wort in boil kettle.

BOIL *(60 minutes)*
- **T-45:** 0.75 oz. Hersbrucker (or equivalent.)
- **T-1:** 1 tablespoon each coriander and bitter orange peel.
- **T-0:** Cool the wort to approximately 95°F, transfer to sanitized fermentor.

FERMENTATION AND BEYOND
- **Lacto fermentation:** 80–90°F for 5–7 days before adding witbier yeast.
- **Sacch fermentation:** 68–70°F for an additional 7–10 days, then package.
- **Serving:** Fresh and lively in a tumbler, shady tree, sunny day.

FARMERS MARKET FRAMBOISE

Targets: **OG:** 1.049, **IBU:** <10, **SRM:** 3.0-5.0, **ABV:** <5.0%

Wild ales + fruit = a beguiling combination. The classic archetype is cherries or raspberries added to a mature lambic to create kriek or framboise, respectively, a sum greater than the whole of its parts. The sourness and earthy fermentation character of the beer harmonize with the fruit's native tannins and acid, while its bright aromatics and flavors surf over the evolving tides of funk.

This is starting to sound like a Parliament concept album, but what we're really embarking on here is a protracted fermentation punctuated by a brew day and a trip to the farmer's market.

If you have a garden or orchard, or know someone who does, even better.

Collect your fruit at the peak of freshness. If the base beer isn't ready to be fruited when you buy or pick the berries, wash them and store in ziplocks in the freezer until it is (we'll need to do this anyway, in order to rupture the fruit cell walls to maximize color and flavor).

The magnificent thing about these beers is that they're actually quite simple—malted barley and raw wheat, plus good fruit at its peak, plus time. Let's get on the mothership.

Illustration by David Witt

SHOPPING LIST

- 6 lbs. Rahr Pilsner malt
- 3 lbs. flaked wheat

- 1 oz. low alpha and/or aged hops

- An all-in-one liquid blend for lambic-style ales—Wyeast 3278, White Labs 655, or equivalent.

- 2.5–3 lbs. fresh raspberries

KEY POINTS FOR KEY PINTS

Other fruit? Maybe raspberries aren't in season, maybe you hate raspberries, maybe you have peaches, grapes, currants, apricots, or cherries at the ready. Adjust the quantity of fruit used based on the intensity of its flavor, acid, and tannin (for example, you'll need a lot more peaches than you would currants), cut up big fruit as needed, and freeze before use.

Get low-alpha hops, ideally way past their peak: Brewers of traditional lambic use old hops that have had all aromatics and alpha acids aged out of them. We are not after IBUs, so hit up your LHBS for some old inventory. If that's not an option, then choose a variety based on lowest AA% (like French Strisselspalt, German Hersbrucker, or Czech Saaz.)

Be patient: The microflora that shape the flavors and aromas of lambic are not on a 21st century schedule. Although the Sacch portion of the fermentation will be over in relatively short order, the acid bacteria and Brett will be slow but thorough and reward patience and non-intervention. Let the beer take a full trip around the sun in primary before adding fruit, then give it a bit longer for flavors to marry before packaging.

BREWING

PREP
- Mill the grains, then heat strike water to approximately 168°F.

MASH & SPARGE
- **Mash rest:** Add all grains to strike water, mix to 154–156°F, and rest for 60 minutes.
- **Mashout:** Heat it to 170°F for 5 minutes.
- Sparge and collect wort in boil kettle.

BOIL *(60 minutes)*
- **T-60:** 0.75 oz. aged hops.
- **T-0:** Cool the wort, transfer to a sanitized fermentor, aerate well, and pitch yeast.

FERMENTATION AND BEYOND
- **Primary fermentation:** 68–70°F for approximately 12–18 months.
- A few days before racking to secondary, wash and freeze the fruit.
- **Secondary fermentation:** Add frozen fruit to a sanitized carboy or bucket, and rack beer in on top of it. Leave beer on fruit for another 1–2 months before packaging.
  Nota bene: If bottle-conditioning, add a bit of fresh ale yeast along with priming sugar to ensure even carbonation.
- **Serving:** Chalice, summer twilight, crickets and/or tree frogs.

HIBISCUS RED

Targets: **OG:** 1.049, **IBU:** 22, **SRM:** 4, **ABV:** 4.8%

Let's get back to basics... and then hit it with hibiscus. A flowering plant native to the tropics, dried hibiscus blossoms are infused to make traditional beverages in Africa, India, Central and South America, and the Caribbean. Hibiscus tea has a deep red color and a tart, cranberry-like flavor—it's often served sweetened with sugar, but we'll sweeten it with sweet, sweet beer.

Because we want our hibiscus ale to taste like, you know, hibiscus, we don't want a lot of strong native flavors from the base beer competing for attention. A simple blonde ale makes a good stage to build on.

If we had to call this something, it would be a Spice/Herb/Vegetable Beer, and that's wide-open category. To paraphrase the BJCP style guidelines, it should be a harmonious marriage of beer and what-have-you, reflecting the character of both the base style and the special ingredient(s). To put it in layperson's terms: if it tastes good, do it.

This vision is a light, refreshing ale with a tart, snappy fruit-like flavor—color within the lines and we'll get exactly that.

But like jazz, this is a genre ripe for improvisation. This recipe could be endlessly modified—in the West Indies, hibiscus tea is often seasoned with ginger, cloves, and nutmeg. Hibiscus and dried chipotle morita chili peppers are a good combo. Scrap the hibiscus and dose the base beer with frozen raspberries and fresh mint.

Go nuts with the aftermarket mods, but start small and sample often. It's easy to increase an additive's level of flavor by adding more or steeping longer, but there's no good fix for too much. Start out with a reasonable dose of flavorings, sample the conditioning beer often as it steeps, and package it when it tastes right to you.

SHOPPING LIST

- 8 lbs. Rahr Pale Ale
- 12 oz. Briess Caramel 10L

- 1 oz. Cascade

- A clean, neutral-flavored ale strain—I'm using Wyeast 1056 American Ale

- Nylon or muslin mesh straining bag
- 6.5 oz. dried hibiscus blossoms (check a health food store, or a Mexican grocery where it may be called "flor de Jamaica")

KEY POINTS FOR KEY PINTS

Mash low! To keep the beer balanced and drinkable, we need a highly fermentable wort.

Manage fermentation for a "clean" beer: A low pitch rate, a too-warm fermentation, and/or oxygen-depleted yeast cells will create flavors and aromas that will not play nicely with our hibiscus. A nice fresh pitch and cool fermentation temps are our friends.

Fermenting in a bucket—pros and cons: A plastic bucket fermentor makes addition and removal of our hibiscus pouch much easier than finagling it through the neck of a carboy. However, the hibiscus may leave some color and aroma in the plastic.

Sink it: Sanitize a few glass marbles, stainless hex nuts, or the like, and place them in the mesh bag with the hibiscus to help keep it submerged.

BREWING

PREP
- Make a yeast starter. On brew day, mill the grains and heat strike water to 165°F.

MASH & SPARGE
- **Mash rest:** Add all grains to strike water, mix to 150-152°F, and rest for 60–90 minutes. Collect and heat sparge water.
- **Mashout:** Heat it to 170°F for 5 minutes.
- Sparge and collect the wort in the boil kettle.

BOIL *(60 minutes)*
- **T-60:** 1 oz. Cascade.
- **T-0:** Cool it, transfer to a sanitized fermentor, aerate well, and pitch yeast.

FERMENTATION AND BEYOND
- **Primary fermentation:** Ideally, max out in the low-to-mid-60s°F to keep esters minimal in the finished beer.
- When the beer has reached terminal gravity (in the neighborhood of 1.010), put the hibiscus in the mesh bag and knot it shut. Bring 1 pint of water to a boil in a small saucepan. Steep the bagged hibiscus for a few minutes to sterilize, then add the mesh bag plus steeping water to the fermentor.
- Sample daily after 1–2 days to avoid overdoing it. Allow the beer to condition on the hibiscus at fermentation temperature until it's to your liking, then package and enjoy.

SAISON FATALII

Targets: **OG:** 1.050, **IBU:** 26–28, **SRM:** 17, **ABV:** 5.7%

In autumn, brewing a pumpkin ale would be an obvious choice. The seasonal synchronicity—not to mention those nutmeg-cinnamon aromatics—would go down nice and easy. But, as Tina Turner said in her talking intro to "Proud Mary," we never do nothing nice and easy.

A few years back, I brought home a fatalii pepper transplant from Seed Savers Exchange in Decorah, Iowa and put it in the garden. Ever since, I'm of the opinion we should be looking to tailgate chili, not pumpkin pie, for an inspirational fall seasonal. We never do gourds, either, Tina Turner. This harvest-beer season, we bring the capsicum, citizens.

Bucking the trend of amber-colored and clean fall seasonals, our base beer will be a pretty simple black saison, with lots of fruity yeast character that can trade riffs with the pepper, and enough heft and gravity to balance the zing of the capsaicin.

As to the profile of the chili pepper, I agree with Scott Russell, who, in an article on the topic in Brew Your Own magazine, wrote: "First and foremost, a chili beer must be a beer. The chili is secondary. The beer itself must be sound, solid, balanced and worth brewing."

Fatalii peppers can bring up to 400,000 Scoville units of mouth-hurt close behind a bright citrus flavor. In keeping with Mr. Russell's precepts, a little will go a long way and discretion is the better part of this saison. We're looking for a citrus pepper flavor integrated with yeast esters and a background murmur of chili heat amidst the soft roastiness of dehusked Perla Negra malt (or at least I am—you can dial it up in your batch, it's your damn beer.)

Fataliis are similar in both flavor and heat level to habaneros, which would probably be the closest substitute, but use whatever chili variety looks good in your garden, root cellar, or co-op. Dried chilis could work, too—the raisiny quality of pasilla or ancho would go nicely with the dark malt, while the sweet cherry tones of tien tsin or chipotle morita would interplay with the yeast.

SHOPPING LIST

- 9 lbs. Belgian Pilsner malt
- 8 oz. Patagonia Perla Negra or Weyermann Carafa Type 1

- 1 oz. German Perle, or equivalent (Hersbrucker, Tettnang, Spalt)

- Wyeast 3711 French Saison—chosen specifically for its tropical fruit/peachy esters to partner up with the bright citrus of fresh fatalii

- 1 fatalii pepper (or the equivalent of your choice)
- ⅓ cup vodka

KEY POINTS FOR KEY PINTS

Less can become more, but not vice versa: Start with just one pepper. It's always possible to add more chilis or extend the secondary to extract more heat, but it's impossible to undo a chili addition so high it makes the beer undrinkable.

Pepper sources: Farmers markets and co-ops are a good source for varieties like fatalii. For dried peppers—including the aforementioned pasilla, ancho, and tien tsin—consult your premiere local spice emporium.

BREWING

PREP
- Prepare a yeast starter. On brew day, mill the grains and heat strike water to 165°F.

MASH & SPARGE
- **Mash rest:** Add all grains to strike water, mix to 151–153°F, and rest for 60–90 minutes. Collect and heat sparge water.
- **Mashout:** Heat it to 170°F for 5 minutes.
- Sparge and collect the wort in the boil kettle.

BOIL *(60 minutes)*
- **T-60:** 1 oz. Perle (or your choice.)
- **T-0:** Cool it, transfer to a sanitized fermentor, aerate well, and pitch yeast.

FERMENTATION AND BEYOND
- **Primary fermentation:** Aim for a maximum temp in the low-to-mid-70s°F.
- When active fermentation is complete, prepare the chili pepper: wash to clean, then make a small incision in the side of the pepper. Soak in ⅓ cup vodka while you sanitize the siphon equipment and secondary fermentor—this will sanitize the pepper, as well as solubilize the hydrophobic capsaicin oils.
  - *Nota bene:* if using a dried pepper, allow for a bit longer soak in the vodka to ensure adequate contact with the surface.
- Dump the pepper, along with the vodka, into the sanitized secondary fermentor, and siphon the beer in after.
- Sample the beer frequently—at least once a week—and siphon it off the pepper as soon as the heat level is to your liking. Stored cool and dark, this beer will drink well for several months, but the pepper flavor will be more apparent while fresh.

GHOST OF KARELIA SAHTI

Targets: **OG:** 1.090–1.100, **IBU:** 5–7, **SRM:** 15, **ABV:** 11.5%

Happy holidays, citizens! Let's gift each other a potent, astoundingly full-bodied and turbid top-fermented beer.

Native to Finland, the roots of sahti go back to the Middle Ages. It is a strong, barleywine-grade ale flavored with juniper, and brewed for village festivals and special occasions, served young in all its hazy, boozy glory. Consumed as fresh as possible, sahti is served at low CO_2 levels—nearly still, with a bit of residual gas from fermentation, or very lightly carbonated—which further enhances the big, slick texture.

Sahti starts with a mix of malted and unmalted grains—primarily barley with a discernible portion of rye, and wheat may also be used. This rustic mash is lautered through a screen of fresh juniper boughs in a troughlike vessel called a kuurna, made from a tree trunk split lengthwise and hollowed out like a canoe. A token hop addition is scattered over the juniper that lines the kuurna. The sap extracted from the juniper in the mash intercedes in the name of balance, helping the slight hop load offset the fat malt character.

A brief boil following the mash is optional; some sahti brewers skip it. The break material that is normally separated out by a 60–90 minute boil means that ludicrous amounts of body-building cereal proteins carry through to the glass, resulting in a worty, viscous density.

Finnish sahti is often fermented with bread yeast and exhibits a dominant banana ester, making it highly reminiscent of weizenbocks. For us, a Bavarian hefeweizen strain is the best substitute—it will give us those pronounced banana aromatics, and will cope better than baker's yeast with a 10 percent ABV.

Fermentation is quick and vigorous—as little as two days, with a week or so of secondary at cellar temperatures (approximately 55°F). Served within a week or two of brewing, there will be quite a bit of suspended yeast in the glass—again, much like a weizenbock.

All this adds up to a spritzy, turbid, warming, and malty special-event beer you could probably stand a fork in.

SHOPPING LIST

- 2.25 lbs. Weyermann Pils
- 8 oz. Weyermann Rye Malt
- 2 oz. Weyermann CaraWheat
- 1 lb. Weyermann Dark Munich
- 4 oz. flaked wheat

- 0.25 oz. homegrown noble-type hops of approximately 3-5 percent alpha acid **or** 0.25 oz. store-bought whole-flower Tettnang or Saaz

- Your choice of Bavarian-style weizen yeast—I'm using Wyeast 3056 Bavarian Wheat Blend

- A large mesh bag that can hold five pounds of grain
- 0.25 oz. dried juniper berries (available at your LHBS)

KEY POINTS FOR KEY PINTS

Low volume: To ensure we polish off an entire batch quickly, you know, out of respect for tradition, this recipe is formulated as a one-gallon brew-in-a-bag batch. For the adventurous and/or determinedly Finnish, scale up as desired.

Homegrown hops: Finnish farmhouse brewers would have used whatever was growing in the neighborhood; a low-alpha, noble-type variety like Mt. Hood, Liberty, Hallertau, etc., would be ideal. Barring that, whole-cone Saaz or Tettnang will do nicely.

Mash low and long for fermentability: Maximizing the amount of short-chain sugars in the wort will help us achieve maximum ABV in minimum time.

Boil or no boil? We're going to incorporate a very short boil just for the sake of microbial stability, but if you prefer to go full Finnish, proceed from mash directly to cooling and pitching.

Plan for lots of krausen: A blow-off hose or oversized fermentor will be our friend.

BREWING

PREP
- Mill the grains. Collect two gallons of strike water and heat to approximately 160°F.

MASH & SPARGE
- **Mash rest:** Fill the mesh bag with the milled grains, hops, and juniper berries. Immerse the bag in the water and swirl to achieve a uniform 148–149°F. Rest for 60–90 minutes.
- Remove the bag (you can wring out the grains to recover more wort if you like) and discard the spent grain, juniper berries, and hops.

BOIL *(Optional: 10–15 minutes, while blasting Sibelius.)*
- **T-0:** Cool it, transfer to a sanitized fermentor, aerate well, and pitch yeast.

FERMENTATION AND BEYOND
- **Primary fermentation:** Aim for 68°F, and let the temperature free-rise during active fermentation.
- When activity subsides or stops, rack to a secondary fermentor and let the green sahti rest for seven days at 55°F.
- Package and carbonate lightly (if desired). Consume right away with friends and family.

ALEHOOFER GRUIT

Targets: **OG:** 1.052–1.054, **IBU:** 0, **SRM:** 4.5, **ABV:** 5.4%

To crib a page from Neil deGrasse Tyson: if the millennia in which humankind has been brewing beer were condensed down into a single 12-month calendar year, then hops would not have come into conventional use until November. From New Year's Day up through at least Halloween, the flavoring of choice for grain-based ferments would have been a blend of botanicals collectively referred to as gruit.

Not that long ago in the grand scheme of things, gruit beer would have filled your mug at the pub or dinner table. Instead of the floral, herbal bite of *Humulus lupulus*, you'd have tasted a sweet-savory-bitter herbal mélange. Medieval European gruit was built around a trifecta of sweet gale, wild rosemary, and yarrow, but could also include ginger, heather, caraway, juniper, and exotic-for-the-era spices like nutmeg, anise, and cinnamon.

Hops swept through Europe during the Middle Ages and had more-or-less supplanted gruit on the continent by the 16th century. The herbal tradition held out longest in England ("ale" in old English indicated an unhopped cereal-based beverage, while "beer" was one with hops—yeast strain didn't enter into it.)

The reasons for gruit's decline were complex; the Catholic Church exerted a virtual monopoly on the control, sale of, and rights to use gruit herbs, so using hops to flavor beer became a politically, economically, and religiously significant act during the Protestant Reformation.

Plus, certain aspects of gruit might have been disagreeable to some Reformers. Beer historian and herbalist Stephen H. Buhner noted that gruit was considered: "highly intoxicating and aphrodisiacal when consumed in sufficient quantity. [It] stimulates the mind, creates euphoria, and enhances sexual drive."

Today gruit is enjoying something of a revival, so let's forage for a local plant that's in abundance around this time of year. Ground ivy, *Glechoma hederacea*, a fragrant member of the mint family, is also known as Creeping Charlie or Creeping Jenny, but to medieval Saxons it was alehoof ("ale herb.") It's easy to find but, obviously, make sure your source hasn't been treated with herbicide or fertilizer.

And with all that said, there ain't nothin' to it but to gruit.

SHOPPING LIST

- 10 lbs. English pale ale malt

- Your favorite ale strain—I'm going with good ol' 1056

- Approximately 6–8 quarts (loosely packed) ground ivy leaves, stems, and/or flowers, well-cleaned

KEY POINTS FOR KEY PINTS

Ferment fast, drink fresh: One unquestionable benefit hops brought to beer was extended shelf life; gruit won't benefit from extended aging.

Alehoof alternates: If you don't want to forage, or can't find an herbicide-free source of ground ivy, feel free to substitute an ounce or two of your own custom blend of dried botanicals from your LHBS, grocery store, or spice cabinet.

BREWING

PREP
- Mill the grains.
- Heat strike water to approximately 165°F.

MASH & SPARGE
- **Mash rest:** Add all grains to strike water, mix to 151–153°F, and rest for 60–90 minutes. Collect and heat sparge water.
- **Mashout:** Heat it to 170°F for 5 minutes.
- Sparge and collect the wort in the boil kettle.

BOIL *(60 minutes, while partying like it's 1066.)*
- **T-60:** Add roughly two-thirds of the ground ivy (or your own mixture.)
- **T-0:** Add the remaining ground ivy at the end of the boil, then cool it, transfer to a sanitized fermentor, aerate well, and pitch yeast.

FERMENTATION AND BEYOND
- **Primary fermentation:** Aim for a maximum temperature in the low-to-mid-60s°F. When activity subsides and gravity is stable, allow a few more days of settling then proceed with packaging.
- Our alehoof gruit is best enjoyed fresh and a bit green, just like the spring.

AULD ALLIANCE PEATED BIÈRE DE GARDE

Targets: **OG:** 1.056–58, **IBU:** 21–22, **SRM:** 7.2, **ABV:** 5.3%

True story: in France, more Scotch whisky is sold in one month than Cognac is sold in a year. Is it a relic of the Auld Alliance, a fetish for something other than brandy and calvados, or something else? Do the French just know a good thing when they see it?

Regardless, the love of pot-distilled, sherry oak-matured malt spirit in that country has been a bellwether for some French brewers as well. The Alsatian brewery Fischer (called Groupe Pêcheur in its home country) was credited by beer writer Michael Jackson with starting the trend of *bières au malt à whisky,* brewed with a proportion of Scottish whisky malt. We'll take inspiration from that to brew an amber autumn-into-winter bière de garde that speaks with a slight peat-smoked accent.

I like to think of bière de garde as a saison seen through the lens of a Bavarian lager brewer—much cleaner, malt-forward, but not totally absent some amount of fermentation character. Like many modern producers, we'll use a lager strain for fermentation but not fuss overmuch about temp control in primary: 65–68°F is *argent liquide.*

A few possible riffs and variations:

- Omit the peated malt and replace 10-20 percent of the Vienna with a beechwood- or -oak smoked malt for a more pervasive but mellower smoke character.
- Goose the gravity and color with 8-12 ounces of dark candi sugar or syrup in the boiler.
- Soak an ounce or two of French medium- or medium-plus toast oak cubes in sherry or port wine for a couple days, then add the cubes to secondary.

SHOPPING LIST

- 10 lbs. Château Vienna
- 2 oz. Simpsons Peated Malt
- 4 oz. Weyermann Carabohemian

- 2 oz. French Strisselspalt

- Wyeast 2112 California Lager, WLP810 San Francisco Lager, or Saflager W-34/70

KEY POINTS FOR KEY PINTS

Moderation is a virtue: Peated malt can become palate-fatiguing, and friends don't let friends over-peat. At the ~1 percent inclusion rate used here, it will be a supporting note—blending in with the scenery and mostly behaving itself.

Unless you really like peat: For fans of aggressive Islay single malts, the amount of peated malt in the grist could be doubled or even tripled, but it will quickly become the center-piece of the finished beer, crowding out the Vienna and color malts and any fermentation character.

Hop substitutes: If Strisselspalt proves hard to source, try Mt. Hood or Crystal.

BREWING

PREP
- Make a yeast starter. On brew day, mill the grains and heat strike water to 165°F.

MASH & SPARGE
- Add all grains to strike water
- **Mash rest:** 151–153°F for 60–90 minutes. Collect and heat sparge water.
- **Mashout:** Heat it to 170°F for 5 minutes.
- Sparge and collect the wort in the boil kettle.

BOIL *(60 minutes, while having a dram of something from the Highlands)*
- **T-60:** 1.5 oz. Strisselspalt.
- **T-0:** Cool it, transfer to a sanitized fermentor, aerate well, and pitch yeast.

FERMENTATION AND BEYOND
- **Primary fermentation:** Aim for a pitching temp of 63–65°F, and a fermentation temp of roughly 65–68°F. When activity begins to slow, allow the fermentor to warm up to around 70°F for a 2–3 day diacetyl rest—14 days, total, depending on yeast and temp.
- Rack to secondary and cool crash. Depending on chosen yeast strain, temperature and other factors, this may take days or weeks. if needed, use a fining like gelatin or Biofine prior to packaging.
- Cork-and-cage finish Belgian-style bottles make for a beautiful presentation, but our peated bière de garde will do great on draft as well.
- This beer will drink well at 6–8 weeks, but will continue to improve and evolve for several months if stored in a dark, cool place.

ORZEL BIALY GRODZISKIE HOPPY SMOKED WHEAT BEER

Targets: **OG:** 1.028, **IBU:** 18-20, **SRM:** 2.5, **ABV:** 2.8%

Smoky, hoppy, 100 percent wheat, and a bantamweight level of alcohol—intrigued?

Grodziskie is an ale indigenous to, and named for, the Polish town of Grodzisk (Germanified to Grätz during its years in the Prussian empire, so you may also find this beer style referred to as Grätzer). It originated in the 16th century and became so internationally renowned that less than 200 years later, Grodzisk supported 53 breweries. Like its cousins Berliner weisse and Gose, Grodziskie essentially died out in the 20th century but has staged a comeback thanks to interest from craft and homebrewers in the US.

Grodziskie's signature ingredient is malted wheat dried in wood-fired kilns, fueled by Poland's primeval oak forests. This creates both a cumulus-like stand of foam and its low-key but not acrid smoky character. The region's minerally, high-sulfate water elevates the impression of bitterness from a couple charges of Saaz-type hops, while a clean-fermenting ale yeast allows these impressions to transmit without interference from esters and phenols.

Illustration by David Witt

SHOPPING LIST

- 5.5 lbs. Weyermann Oak-Smoked Wheat Malt
- 8 oz. rice hulls or oat hulls (add directly to mash—do not mill)

- 1 oz. Polish Lublin or Czech Kazbek

- A clean German ale strain—Wyeast 1007, White Labs 029, or Safale K-97

KEY POINTS FOR KEY PINTS

Oak-smoked wheat: Weyermann is the maltster of record for an authentic Grodziskie. Their oak-smoked wheat malt has a mellow, warm and woodsy campfire quality that's quite unlike the smoky-bacon-ham character of the beechwood-smoked Bamberg Rauchbiers with which you may be more familiar.

Minerally water: The well water in Grodzisk is high in calcium, sulfate, and carbonate, which enhances the perception of bitterness and dryness in the beer. Depending on your brewing water, additions of gypsum and/or calcium carbonate might be beneficial.

Clean-fermenting ale yeast: Phenolic and fruity weissbier strains are out of place here—opt instead for an Alt- or Kölsch-style yeast, or, in a pinch, a neutral American ale strain.

Clarification: Per the BJCP guidelines, Grodziskie has "excellent clarity," but with a grist of 100 percent wheat and a frequently non-flocculent strain, there's quite the potential for haze. Filtration, cold-crashing the fermentor (below 40°F is ideal) once fermentation is complete, and/or using some finings like gelatin or Biofine, can help us make a clear beer.

High carbonation: Back in the day, Grodziskie was euphemistically called "Polish Champagne" (presumably by Prussians or residents of one of the many countries to which the ale was exported in its heyday...the records are mumbly) due in part to its pale color and clarity, but primarily its effervescence. When it comes time to carbonate, aim for 3 volumes of CO_2 for a very sparkling presentation with big foam.

BREWING

PREP
- Mill the wheat malt, then heat strike water to approximately 164°F

MASH & SPARGE
- **Mash rest:** Add wheat malt to strike water, mix to 152-154°F, and rest for 60 minutes.
- Add the rice hulls once mash rest is complete. Collect and heat sparge water.
- **Mashout:** Heat it to 170°F for 5 minutes.
- Sparge and collect wort in boil kettle.

BOIL *(60 minutes)*
- **T-60:** 0.75 oz. Lublin (or Kazbek.)
- **T-30:** 0.25 oz. Lublin (or Kazbek.)
- **T-0:** Cool the wort and transfer to a sanitized fermentor, aerate well, and pitch yeast.

FERMENTATION AND BEYOND
- **Primary fermentation:** 62-66°F for approximately 7-10 days.
- **Secondary fermentation (optional, for aiding clarification):** 40°F for 7-14 days
- **Serving:** Footed Pilsner glass, plate of pierogies, Polish horseshoes.

Michael Dawson is a longtime homebrewer and 20-year veteran of the beer industry. He was a founding member of the webcast "Brewing TV" and sits on the editorial review board for *BYO Magazine*. A BJCP-certified judge since 1998, Dawson has authored articles on beer for several local and national publications including *The Growler Magazine*, where he's been the resident homebrew columnist since 2012.

Illustration by David Witt

INGREDIENTS

ADDITIVES

SUGARS

PROCESSES